Managing Conditional Access and Compliance with Intune

Intune Playbook Companion Series

Dr. Patrick Jones

OLYMPUS ACADEMY
PRESS

After finishing this book, if you are keen to deepen your knowledge of Intune, you have several options:

- Supplement your learning with other books in the Intune Playbook Companion Series

- Contact Dr. Patrick Jones for information about professional service opportunities

- Check out the online Intune Basics course provided by Olympus Academy, which includes detailed instructions and video tutorials.

Bit.ly/intunebasics

Thank you for supporting this publication and enjoy your learning!

Table of Contents

Welcome to the World of Compliance and Access Control with Microsoft Intune.

In today's technology-driven environment, data has become one of the most valuable assets for businesses of all sizes. The ability to access information from anywhere in the world and on any device has changed the way organizations operate, but it has also introduced new challenges. Cyber threats and data breaches pose serious risks to company reputation, financial stability, and legal standing. As a result, maintaining robust security measures and meeting compliance requirements has become a top priority for IT professionals. The modern digital landscape demands that businesses not only store and process data securely, but also ensure that they are prepared to respond to ever-evolving threats.

Microsoft Intune plays a pivotal role in this balancing act by providing a centralized way to manage devices, applications, and policies across your organization. Whether your workforce uses laptops, smartphones, or tablets, Intune helps you maintain control over how devices access corporate data. By enforcing compliance settings—ranging from password requirements to operating system updates—Intune ensures that each device aligns with your company's security standards. Conditional access then takes this protection a step further, restricting or allowing access to data based on real-time risk assessments. Together, compliance and conditional access provide a two-pronged approach: one sets the rules, and the other decides who can pass through the gates based on those rules.

Imagine a small but growing firm called 365 Strategies that has employees scattered across different regions. Some team members are in the office, while others work from home or travel to meet clients. They all need quick access to confidential marketing data, client information, and internal communication platforms. Before using Intune, 365 Strategies struggled with managing different device types, each with its

1

own security quirks. Laptops were missing important updates because employees postponed them, and mobile devices were connecting to public Wi-Fi networks without any additional security checks. When a contract was on the line and a device got infected with malware, the team realized how devastating a single security lapse could be for the company's reputation.

By implementing Intune for both compliance and conditional access, 365 Strategies found a solution. Not only were they able to establish clear guidelines for device configurations, but they also set up rules to quickly quarantine any device that displayed suspicious behavior. This means that the marketing team could focus on creativity and client work, knowing that their data was protected by enterprise-grade security policies, even if they were working at a café or an airport lounge. The leadership could rest easier, too, because compliance reports and real-time dashboards gave them an at-a-glance view of the organization's security posture.

This book will guide you through the essential aspects of setting up compliance policies and configuring conditional access with Intune, all while keeping the process approachable. By understanding both the technical details and the strategic reasons behind these features, you'll be able to tailor your Intune environment to your unique business needs. So let's begin this journey, exploring the robust capabilities of Intune and learning how to defend your data in an ever-changing digital world.

Chapter 1: The Foundations of Compliance Policies

The modern workplace is at once a conduit for unprecedented innovation and a battleground for digital threats. Data flows smoothly across networks, devices, and geographic boundaries, offering businesses the agility they need to compete. But with this agility comes a responsibility to secure that data and uphold certain standards—legal, ethical, and operational. This responsibility is the cornerstone of compliance. While some might equate "compliance" with elaborate regulation and red tape, effective compliance policies are what ensure that data remains protected, organizations stay out of legal jeopardy, and employees can perform their work free from cybersecurity crises. In the realm of Microsoft Intune, compliance policies take center stage as the guiding principles that define and enforce how devices should operate within corporate environments.

To understand why compliance policies are so central to Intune, it helps to grasp the broader context of device management in a cloud-centric world. Traditionally, organizations governed their security posture with on-premises tools and perimeter-based defenses—firewalls, intrusion detection systems, and locked-down network segments. Those measures were effective when employees worked mainly from company-issued desktops connected to a single corporate network. However, times have changed dramatically. The number of remote workers has grown, personal devices are used for business more than ever, and enterprises of all sizes rely heavily on cloud services. These changes bring enormous convenience and cost savings, but they also expand the attack surface. A device's security can be compromised in countless ways, from outdated operating systems to employees unwittingly connecting to malicious public Wi-Fi networks. Given these risks, organizations need a flexible, intelligent way to ensure each device adheres to security standards—no matter where it resides.

This is where compliance policies step in. At its simplest, a compliance policy is a set of rules that devices must follow to be deemed secure by the organization. For example, a policy might mandate that a Windows laptop be encrypted and have a strong password. Another policy might require a mobile phone running iOS or Android to have a specific minimum operating system version. If a device meets these requirements, it's marked as "compliant." If it falls short, the system can restrict access to corporate data until the device is brought up to standard. While the concept is simple—ensure devices are secure before granting them corporate privileges—it's not always easy to implement. Different platforms behave differently, and updates to operating systems can shift security capabilities in ways that might break older policies. Moreover, people are at the heart of any compliance strategy: they must be informed, guided, and encouraged to follow best practices.

Microsoft Intune makes this process more manageable by consolidating policy creation, assignment, and monitoring within a single administrative interface. Instead of juggling multiple disparate tools—one for Windows, one for mobile operating systems—administrators can build compliance rules for a variety of device types under the umbrella of Intune. This not only streamlines management but also provides a consistent source of truth: a single repository where you can quickly check whether devices meet company standards, which rules they might be violating, and how to guide users to fix any issues. Intune's reporting capabilities play a major role here, providing organizations with the data they need to see trends or identify problem areas in real time. Without this level of visibility, an organization might only learn about a major vulnerability once it has already been exploited, making remediation costly and potentially damaging to both revenue and reputation.

Equally important is the notion that compliance is more than just a security checkbox. In many industries, external regulations—like HIPAA for healthcare, GDPR for data protection in the European Union, or PCI-DSS for payment card security—require proof that an organization is taking steps to protect sensitive information. While Intune doesn't eliminate the complexity of these regulations outright, it offers a structured approach to fulfilling them. Admins can define policies that align with the specific standards required. For instance, if GDPR necessitates certain encryption levels for data stored on mobile devices, Intune compliance policies can enforce encryption on all devices that handle personal information. The ability to generate reports showing which devices meet these criteria, and which do not, is invaluable should an organization need to demonstrate compliance to regulators, auditors, or clients.

Moreover, compliance policies form the bedrock for conditional access, which is covered in-depth later in this book. Conditional access is the logic gate that checks whether a device complies with policies, then decides if it can connect to certain applications or data. Without well-crafted compliance policies, conditional access would be based on guesswork, or it might rely on more superficial checks like user credentials alone. When compliance policies are robust, conditional access can be precise, granting access only to devices that truly meet the organization's security and regulatory standards. This synergy—where compliance sets the rules and conditional access enforces them—provides a powerful mechanism for securing data in a zero-trust world.

Zero trust is a security model you will hear frequently in discussions about modern cyber defense. It operates on the principle that no device or identity is inherently trustworthy simply because it resides on a "secure" network. Every access request is continuously verified. Compliance policies feed directly into this model by supplying the criteria that define whether a device is trustworthy at any given moment. If a laptop is missing a critical security patch, the policy detects non-compliance, and conditional access might block that laptop from sensitive resources. Even if the user has the right credentials, the device fails the trust test. While this might seem strict, it's a necessary measure in an era where user credentials alone are no longer sufficient for preventing breaches.

Historically, organizations that tried to enforce device compliance without a unified solution like Intune faced a litany of challenges. They might have used group policy objects in Windows environments for desktops, separate mobile device management solutions for smartphones, and manual checks for certain legacy systems. This patchwork approach often resulted in inconsistent compliance standards, as each platform had its own limitations and separate reporting systems. Because security is only as strong as its weakest link, a single misconfigured platform could give attackers a foot in the door. The consolidation that Intune offers, therefore, is not just about convenience; it's a strategic advantage that helps administrators maintain a holistic security stance.

The concept of compliance also extends beyond technical settings to people and processes. A policy isn't merely a set of toggles in the Intune dashboard; it's a reflection of an organization's risk tolerance, business goals, and corporate culture. For example, a company with a high tolerance for risk might allow personal devices to connect to certain applications without stringent checks, perhaps for reasons of employee productivity. Another organization that deals with sensitive data—like a law firm or hospital—may choose stricter policies. Each compliance policy effectively becomes a microcosm of the organization's values: do we prioritize convenience over security, or vice versa? Are we willing to block user access if they fail to apply an operating system patch on time, or do we prefer to send repeated reminders before finally restricting access?

This decision-making process, in many ways, underscores why compliance cannot be an afterthought. The foundations laid out in policies will influence day-to-day operations, from how frequently devices update to how users sign in. A well-crafted set of guidelines can minimize disruptions by guiding employees toward best practices. For instance, a policy might nudge users to enable multi-factor authentication or require them to install certain security applications. These steps reduce the risk of data breaches, but they also place demands on users, who must adapt to new routines. Good communication and training, therefore, become part of the compliance journey. Administrators who treat policies as purely technical configurations, without explaining their purpose, risk facing confusion or pushback from employees. In contrast, clearly communicating the "why" behind each policy fosters a sense of shared responsibility for security.

As we venture deeper into this book, you'll notice that many aspects of Intune's compliance features build upon these foundational ideas. You'll learn how to craft policies for diverse device types, assign them to the right sets of users, and monitor the results. We'll explore how to strike the right balance between robust security measures and the practical realities of day-to-day business operations. Ultimately, this first chapter is intended to prime you for the chapters ahead, where you'll get hands-on with policy creation, troubleshooting, and advanced strategies like conditional access. By keeping the core principles of compliance at the forefront—namely, that it's an ongoing process requiring both technical and human considerations—you'll be better prepared to make the most of Intune's capabilities.

Compliance policies serve as the backbone of a secure digital environment by enforcing standards that keep data safe and operations consistent. Their relevance extends across all industries, whether you're working in healthcare, finance, retail, or technology. By providing clarity on how devices should be configured and what is expected of users, compliance policies help organizations navigate a complex threat landscape while meeting regulatory obligations. As a crucial part of the Microsoft Intune ecosystem, these policies integrate seamlessly with the other security tools in your arsenal, enabling you to manage endpoints holistically. In the coming chapters, we'll expand on how to implement, customize, and maintain these policies in real-world scenarios. For now, it's enough to understand that compliance isn't merely about avoiding fines or passing audits—it's about establishing a culture of security that protects your organization's most valuable assets: its data, its people, and its reputation.

Chapter 2: Introducing Microsoft Intune

What is Microsoft Intune?

In an age when employees can work from anywhere, on any device, organizations need a way to protect their data without sacrificing flexibility. This challenge has given rise to mobile device management (MDM) and mobile application management (MAM) solutions that enable IT departments to define and enforce security standards, no matter where their users happen to be. Microsoft Intune sits firmly within this domain, offering organizations a cloud-based service that simplifies how they manage apps, devices, and data. Whether it's safeguarding company email, rolling out new applications, or ensuring that a user's device meets established security requirements, Intune provides a single interface to coordinate all these tasks.

To understand Intune's true scope, it helps to see how it evolved. Initially launched under different branding, Microsoft's vision for Intune has matured significantly over time, especially as organizations started relying more on mobile and cloud technologies. Today, Intune is a core part of Microsoft Endpoint Manager—a unified platform that encompasses multiple tools for managing endpoints, including devices running Windows, iOS, Android, and even macOS. In practical terms, what this means is that Intune is not just an add-on feature or a small module tucked away in a larger suite. Instead, it occupies center stage, playing a pivotal role in how organizations configure, protect, and monitor the devices their employees use every day.

At its heart, Intune is a cloud service. There's no requirement to run servers on-premises or maintain separate infrastructure to make it work. The administrative console itself is web-based, accessed through the Microsoft Endpoint Manager admin center. This design offers an immediate advantage: administrators can log in from anywhere to check device compliance, deploy new apps, or troubleshoot user issues. As long as you have an internet connection and proper credentials, you can manage the entire device ecosystem without being physically tied to a corporate data center. This also means that updates to Intune happen automatically on Microsoft's backend. You don't have to worry about manually patching servers or scheduling downtime to upgrade your management platform; you receive the latest features and improvements as soon as Microsoft releases them.

When people hear "device management," they often picture basic tasks like provisioning laptops or pushing security policies to smartphones. However, Intune goes beyond these basics by integrating seamlessly with the rest of the Microsoft ecosystem, especially Azure Active Directory (Azure AD). Azure AD serves as the identity backbone for countless Microsoft services—Office 365, Dynamics 365, and others—and it's also the repository where you manage user identities, groups, and authentication rules. By leveraging Azure AD, Intune inherits robust identity features such as multi-factor authentication, role-based access control, and conditional access. This deep integration means that when a device enrolls in Intune, it can immediately enforce relevant security measures, aligning with a "zero trust" philosophy that demands continuous verification of users and devices.

One of the clearest benefits of Intune being cloud-based is how quickly it can scale. If you're running a small pilot program with just a handful of devices, Intune works smoothly. If you need to expand management to thousands or even tens of thousands of devices across multiple geographic locations, Intune can accommodate that growth without requiring any extra hardware. Microsoft's global infrastructure does the heavy lifting, allowing organizations to focus on policy creation and enforcement rather than capacity planning. This elasticity is particularly attractive to companies with fluctuating workforces, such as those that hire seasonal staff or rely on contractors. The overhead of spinning up or shutting down a device management infrastructure is effectively minimized, thanks to the subscription-based, cloud-native model.

When it comes to the breadth of functionality within Intune, most administrators break it down into two core areas: MDM and MAM. MDM capabilities revolve around managing a device's overall configuration, security posture, and access to corporate resources. For instance, you might set a device lock policy to ensure that a user's phone locks after a certain period of inactivity, or you might enforce encryption requirements to protect data in case the device is lost or stolen. MAM, on the other hand, focuses on the applications and data running on the device rather than the device itself. A classic scenario is allowing employees to use their personal smartphones for work (often referred to as "Bring Your Own Device" or BYOD). Rather than locking down the entire phone, which might frustrate users and intrude on their personal space, MAM policies allow you to secure and manage only the work-related applications, such as Outlook, Teams, or Word. This approach keeps personal data separate and preserves the user's autonomy, while still giving the organization control over its sensitive information.

In practice, Intune's MDM and MAM features complement each other. An organization might choose to enroll corporate-owned devices into MDM for full control, while letting employees with personal devices use MAM-based policies to protect corporate apps. This level of flexibility is what sets Intune apart: it acknowledges that not all devices and not all use cases are the same. Some scenarios warrant strict device-level controls, while others benefit from a more nuanced app-centric approach. The administrator's role then becomes one of carefully designing which policies apply to which set of users or devices, striking a balance between security and user experience.

The question "Where does Intune fit into Microsoft Endpoint Manager?" often arises because "Microsoft Endpoint Manager" is a relatively new name within Microsoft's rebranding efforts. Microsoft Endpoint Manager serves as an overarching solution that brings together several key components: Microsoft Intune for cloud-based management, Configuration Manager (commonly known as ConfigMgr or SCCM) for on-premises device management, and co-management capabilities that bridge both environments. Essentially, Microsoft Endpoint Manager provides a unified admin experience: you log into one console where you can see all your devices—cloud-managed or otherwise—and take actions like deploying apps, managing updates, or defining compliance policies. This means organizations transitioning from a traditional on-premises model to a cloud-based one can do so gradually. They can move some devices to Intune while keeping others managed by Configuration Manager, all under the same administrative umbrella. Eventually, many organizations do go fully cloud with Intune, but the co-management path provides a smoother migration experience.

It's also important to realize that Intune isn't an isolated point solution; it works in tandem with other Microsoft security tools. For example, Microsoft Defender for Endpoint offers advanced threat detection and response capabilities. If Defender detects that a device is compromised or at high risk, it can share that information with Intune, and Intune can mark the device as non-compliant. This synergy closes the loop between detecting threats and taking action, ensuring that potentially dangerous devices are quarantined before they can access sensitive corporate resources. Similarly, Intune integrates with Microsoft 365 Apps, allowing administrators to deploy Office applications to managed devices, control who can use them, and ensure they're kept up to date with the latest security patches. This holistic approach to device and app management is part of Microsoft's broader strategy: to offer a comprehensive endpoint security and productivity environment under one umbrella.

Given these extensive capabilities, the next question is often about costs and licensing. Intune is available either as a standalone subscription or bundled in various Microsoft licensing packages, such as Microsoft 365 E3, E5, or specific "Business" licenses. This flexibility allows small businesses, large enterprises, and everything in between to tailor their licensing strategy to their needs. Some organizations discover they already have Intune included in their existing Microsoft 365 license, meaning they can start using it right away without any additional expense. For others, adopting Intune may involve strategic budgeting to ensure they can leverage all the services they need—be it Intune alone or the entire Microsoft Endpoint Manager suite.

The significance of Intune becomes even more apparent when organizations consider the broader landscape of cybersecurity. Cyber threats are ever-evolving, with attackers employing sophisticated tactics to compromise devices. Whether these tactics involve phishing attempts that harvest login credentials or malware targeting known software vulnerabilities, organizations need a multi-layered defense. Having a device management solution like Intune at the foundation means there is a systematic approach to security and compliance: devices are enrolled, their statuses are tracked, and any that deviate from security baselines can be flagged and remediated. More advanced layers—like conditional access policies that base access decisions on real-time risk assessments—then build upon this foundation. At the end of the day, Intune is not just a tool for administrators to tick boxes on a compliance checklist; it's a platform that binds together identity, devices, and apps in a secure ecosystem.

When people outside of IT think about "managing devices," they often picture an invasive scenario: an overbearing corporate policy that forces reboots at inconvenient times, or locks out certain device features. While it's certainly possible to misconfigure or overreach with Intune, Microsoft has designed the service to be as user-friendly as it is admin-friendly. Much of the user experience depends on the specific policies an organization chooses to implement. With the right balance, end users may barely notice that Intune is running on their devices. They might simply see an unobtrusive app enrollment process, followed by occasional prompts to update a passcode or install a recommended application. This means companies can maintain robust security without hampering productivity or irritating employees—an all-too-common problem with heavy-handed security tools in the past.

Microsoft Intune is a robust, cloud-based service for managing devices and applications that has become indispensable in the modern workplace. By centralizing policy creation, deployment, and monitoring, Intune gives administrators the visibility and control they need to protect company data. It offers the flexibility of both device-level (MDM) and app-level (MAM) management, integrates seamlessly with Azure Active Directory for identity-based security measures, and fits neatly into the broader Microsoft Endpoint Manager ecosystem for unified endpoint management. Whether you're running a handful of corporate-issued devices or overseeing a sprawling global fleet of diverse device types,

Intune scales to meet your needs. More than just a set of technical controls, it's a strategic service that influences how employees work, how organizations respond to threats, and how compliance requirements are fulfilled in an increasingly regulated digital environment.

Why Intune Matters for Compliance and Access Control

In today's world of expanding remote work, ever-growing sets of mobile devices, and increasingly stringent data regulations, organizations need solutions that can protect sensitive information without stifling productivity. Microsoft Intune, operating under the broader Microsoft Endpoint Manager umbrella, has emerged as a linchpin in the race to secure modern workplaces. Its core functionality revolves around mobile device management (MDM) and mobile application management (MAM), but beyond those key features, one of the critical reasons Intune matters is its ability to enforce compliance policies and support conditional access. Combined, these two areas form the defensive and offensive lines of a well-rounded security strategy. Compliance policies act as the defensive mechanism—defining the security baselines and settings devices must meet—while conditional access offensively determines who or what gains entry to your organization's data at any given time. The synergy between these components allows organizations to adopt a proactive, zero-trust posture that keeps evolving threats at bay.

To appreciate how Intune enforces compliance policies, it's helpful to think about the phrase "security is only as strong as its weakest link." In many organizations, that weakest link could be a single device—perhaps a personal phone with outdated software or a laptop missing vital patches. If such a device connects freely to corporate resources, an attacker could exploit that device's vulnerabilities, potentially gaining a foothold into the broader network. Intune addresses this risk by providing administrators with a centralized set of controls to define what "compliant" looks like. A compliance policy might, for instance, require encryption on Windows or macOS laptops, enforce minimum OS versions on iOS or Android devices, and mandate password complexity across all device types. Once these rules are in place, Intune continuously checks whether the enrolled devices satisfy these criteria. If a device fails—for example, because the user never turned on encryption or is running an old operating system—Intune flags that device as non-compliant. With that single label, administrators and automated systems can immediately see where the shortfalls lie and take action.

That action is where conditional access comes into play. Think of conditional access as the digital equivalent of a security checkpoint at a major event. While compliance determines what is necessary to pass through the checkpoint—like having a valid ID, not carrying prohibited items, and following certain dress codes—conditional access decides who actually gets waved through and who is turned away at the gate. Once Intune assigns a compliance status to a device, Azure Active Directory (Azure AD) checks that status whenever the user attempts to access corporate applications, email, documents, or other sensitive resources. If the device is marked compliant, the user gains entry with minimal hassle. If the device is non-compliant, the user might be denied or prompted to remediate the issue immediately. This real-time interplay between Intune and Azure AD ensures that only healthy, up-to-date, and properly secured devices can access company data.

From an administrative perspective, the enforcement of compliance policies through Intune offers a high degree of flexibility. For some organizations, the right approach is a strict one: any device that fails compliance gets instantly blocked. Others may adopt a more lenient model, allowing a brief grace period during which employees can correct the issues on their devices before losing access. The objective here is not to punish users but to provide them with clear guidance on how to meet security standards. For example, if an Android phone is running an outdated OS, Intune can send a notification prompting the user to update. While the user is in the process of updating, conditional access might temporarily restrict access to highly sensitive applications, but still allow partial access to other less critical apps. This nuanced enforcement mechanism helps maintain both security and productivity, as employees are more likely to comply if the steps to regain full access are straightforward and well-communicated.

Another significant reason why Intune matters for compliance and access control is its ability to handle the growing phenomenon of Bring Your Own Device (BYOD). Many modern employees prefer using personal smartphones and tablets for work because they are already familiar with their chosen devices and can stay productive anywhere. Although BYOD policies bring obvious advantages in terms of user satisfaction and reduced hardware costs, they also pose a conundrum: how do you protect corporate data on personal devices without invading users' privacy? Intune solves this by separating personal information from corporate applications through mobile application management. Compliance can focus on the security posture of business apps, ensuring they're protected with app-level controls like encryption and password requirements, while leaving an individual's personal data—such as photos, messages, and browsing history—untouched. This dual approach is appealing to both IT and end users, as it meets corporate security demands while respecting personal boundaries. Conditional access further refines this process by granting or denying access to corporate services based on app-level compliance, rather than entire device configurations.

For organizations concerned about regulatory standards such as HIPAA, GDPR, or PCI-DSS, Intune's role in compliance can be a game-changer. Auditors often require evidence that the organization has the capability to enforce data protection measures across all devices. Intune provides tangible proof in the form of reports and real-time dashboards, which show exactly which devices comply with specific rules at any moment. Should an auditor ask to see evidence that all devices storing customer credit card information are encrypted, Intune can quickly generate a report. Moreover, because Intune integrates with Azure AD's conditional access, you can automatically block any device lacking the necessary encryption from accessing data. This automated enforcement loop both enhances security and simplifies regulatory reporting, putting administrators in a stronger position when proving alignment with external standards.

Beyond the realm of regulatory compliance, Intune is also beneficial for day-to-day operational efficiency. Without a centralized management tool, an organization might scramble to address vulnerabilities each time a new bug surfaces or a fresh operating system update emerges. Intune streamlines this process by letting administrators set up baseline configurations and security parameters once, then automatically apply them across the entire device fleet. This capability is particularly useful when zero-day vulnerabilities come to light. If a sudden threat requires a patch, administrators can push that update or enforce a policy that mandates the patch, thereby minimizing the window of exposure. At the same time, conditional access policies ensure that unpatched devices are either barred from critical systems or quarantined in a limited environment. This combination of compliance and access control allows for a rapid, coordinated response to emergent threats.

For smaller organizations, or those with limited IT resources, Intune's cloud-based nature removes much of the overhead typically associated with managing an enterprise security tool. There is no need to set up specialized servers or manage complex on-premises systems; all the configuration is done through the Microsoft Endpoint Manager admin center, which is accessible through a web browser. This simplicity extends to conditional access as well, where administrators define rules using intuitive language like "Require compliant devices" or "Block legacy authentication methods." Once these rules are in place, Azure AD and Intune work together behind the scenes to enforce them. The less time IT teams spend wrestling with infrastructure, the more time they can devote to strategic security initiatives, user training, and overall innovation.

Another benefit that often goes overlooked is how Intune's compliance and conditional access framework seamlessly integrates with other Microsoft security solutions, such as Microsoft Defender for Endpoint. When a potential threat is detected on a user's device, Defender for Endpoint can share that information with Intune, automatically labeling the device as high risk. Intune, in turn, can feed that risk assessment into conditional access policies, which then restrict access to sensitive corporate data. This closed-loop integration transforms a simple alert into a dynamic system that actively protects resources by restricting potentially compromised devices in real time. Instead of relying on manual intervention, the system itself enforces security policies in a swift, consistent manner.

Beyond technical merits, there's also an important human element at play. Security policies that are too rigid or that significantly disrupt a user's workflow can lead to pushback and attempts to bypass controls. On the other hand, if security measures are too lax, organizations leave themselves open to unnecessary risk. Intune's approach to compliance and conditional access attempts to strike a balance. Users are given clarity about what is required of their devices, and the process to remediate compliance issues is usually straightforward—update an OS, enable disk encryption, install a mandatory app, or modify a password setting. When users know exactly what they need to do, and when they see that the rules are enforced fairly and consistently, they are far more likely to cooperate.

Ultimately, the reason Intune matters for compliance and access control is that it weaves these concerns into every layer of device and user management. Security is no longer just an afterthought or a separate requirement; it's built into how devices enroll, how they access data, and how they remain in good standing as part of an organization's broader security ecosystem. By linking compliance statuses directly to conditional access decisions, Intune ensures that security standards aren't just guidelines on paper—they're active, enforced policies. The result is a system in which the moment a device strays from compliance standards, the appropriate enforcement actions are taken automatically.

As we navigate further into this book, the deeper details of configuring compliance rules and setting up conditional access will become clearer. You'll learn how to structure these policies to align with your organization's specific security needs, whether that means focusing on encryption, OS versions, multi-factor authentication, or all of the above.

You'll see examples of how device enrollment works in practice, how to monitor for compliance, and what happens when devices fail. And you'll come to appreciate how conditional access is more than just a binary allow-or-block system—it can be finely tuned to adapt access controls based on risk, user behavior, and contextual factors like location. Ultimately, Intune's importance in this conversation goes far beyond mere configuration settings; it shapes the entire philosophy of how an organization approaches device management and security. By automating compliance checks and integrating those checks into access decisions, Intune streamlines a once-laborious process and makes modern security both sustainable and adaptable, even in the face of evolving threats.

Chapter 3: Understanding Compliance Policies in Intune

Creating Compliance Policies

Designing and implementing compliance policies in Intune is at the very heart of securing your organization's devices. These policies outline the minimum requirements each device must meet to be considered safe for accessing corporate data. They allow administrators to define specific rules for areas like password complexity, operating system versions, and device encryption. The power of compliance policies lies not just in the rules themselves, but in the automated checks Intune performs to ensure each enrolled device follows those rules. When a device falls short, Intune flags it as non-compliant, setting the stage for actions such as sending alerts, blocking access to corporate resources, or guiding users through remediation steps. This methodical approach to security replaces guesswork with consistent, enforceable standards—key to scaling device management across various environments and device types.

A compliance policy typically begins its life in the Microsoft Endpoint Manager admin center, where administrators define the scope, settings, and assignment of the policy. The admin center acts as the command hub, offering a straightforward interface in which you can create and edit policies for different platforms like Windows, iOS, and Android. Although there may be slight variations in the exact controls and configurations for each platform, the underlying philosophy remains constant: determine what "secure" looks like in your organization, then let Intune do the heavy lifting to confirm whether devices meet that definition.

Step-by-Step Guide to Setting Up Compliance Policies

1. **Accessing the Admin Center**
   The process begins by navigating to the Microsoft Endpoint Manager admin center, usually accessed through the Azure portal or by going directly to endpoint.microsoft.com. Once you log in

with the appropriate credentials, you are presented with a dashboard that displays the overall status of enrolled devices, app deployments, and security alerts. From this dashboard, locate the section dedicated to Devices. This area allows you to manage not only compliance but also device enrollment, configuration profiles, and a range of security settings.

2. **Navigating to Compliance Policies**
Within the Devices section, there is a subsection labeled Compliance policies. Selecting it reveals existing policies, if any have been created before, or shows an empty list if you are starting from scratch. The main page typically provides a quick overview of policy names, platforms targeted, and deployment statuses. This overview lets administrators quickly see which policies are active, how many devices are targeted, and whether any policies might be outdated or conflicting with others.

3. **Initiating Policy Creation**
To create a new policy, you usually click an option like + Create policy. Intune then asks you to select a platform, such as Windows 10 and later, iOS/iPadOS, or Android. While the overall approach is consistent, this initial choice determines which device-specific settings and rules will be available. For instance, Windows-based policies might include options for BitLocker encryption, whereas Android policies might focus on requiring a minimum OS version or enabling device encryption differently.

4. **Defining Basic Information**
After choosing the platform, Intune prompts you to enter a name and description for your new compliance policy. These fields might seem trivial, but a clear naming convention can save significant time when troubleshooting or reviewing your security posture weeks or months later. You might choose something descriptive like "Windows 10 – Minimum OS and Encryption Policy" or "iOS – Secure Work Profile Requirements." The description can detail the purpose of the policy, its creation date,

and any other contextual information that could help another administrator understand its intent.

5. **Configuring Compliance Settings**

   Once you've specified the basic information, you proceed to the heart of the policy: defining the compliance rules. Each platform provides a selection of possible requirements. For Windows devices, you may enforce BitLocker encryption, mandate secure boot, or set password lengths and complexity. On Android, you might require device encryption as well, dictate screen-lock requirements, and ensure that devices run a minimum OS version. For iOS, Intune can verify the OS version, enforce a device passcode, and block devices that are jailbroken. Depending on your organization's security needs, you can mix and match various settings. The key here is striking a balance between a robust security stance and a feasible user experience. If you are too lax, your organization is at risk; if you are too strict, users may find it difficult to stay in compliance, leading to high volumes of help desk tickets and frustration.

6. **Specifying Actions for Non-Compliance**

   Further along in the setup, you decide what should happen when a device fails to meet any of the defined criteria. For example, you may configure Intune to mark the device as non-compliant immediately and potentially block access to specific apps or data. Alternatively, you could set up a grace period, giving employees a few days to fix the issue before more serious actions take place. This flexibility is useful if your policy changes often, or if you want to ensure users aren't abruptly locked out of their devices without warning. Some organizations choose to send out automated emails or push notifications, giving employees instructions on how to address the compliance gap. This approach fosters collaboration between IT and end users, making the security process more transparent and manageable.

7. **Reviewing and Assigning the Policy**

   Once you finish configuring the settings, the next step is

reviewing your choices and assigning the policy to the relevant groups of devices or users. Intune's assignment model allows you to target specific Azure AD groups, which might be based on department, job role, or device ownership (corporate-owned versus BYOD). This ensures that the right compliance standards apply to the right set of devices. For instance, you might have a stricter policy for devices used by executive leadership or for those handling highly sensitive financial data. Conversely, devices used primarily for basic communication might have a more relaxed set of rules. Taking time to define these Azure AD groups accurately can help you segment your device landscape, making compliance targeting far more efficient.

8. **Monitoring and Testing**

   After assigning your policy, Intune offers various reporting tools to monitor compliance status across the organization. It's wise to test the new policy on a small group of pilot devices before rolling it out broadly. This testing phase can reveal unintended issues—like a requirement that conflicts with a critical business app—or highlight areas where user communication might need improvement. Once any adjustments are made, you can proceed with broader deployment, confident that the policy will perform as intended.

Policy Settings for Different Device Platforms

Although many core ideas remain the same across platforms, each type of device—Windows, iOS, and Android—comes with its own nuances. A single organization can easily manage a mix of these platforms, making it important to understand how settings differ. The details below offer a glimpse into the specifics you might encounter.

Windows Devices

When creating a compliance policy for Windows 10 or 11, you can focus on elements like encryption status, secure boot, and health attestation. BitLocker encryption is commonly enforced so that data remains protected even if a device is lost or stolen. Secure boot ensures that the device starts up using only software trusted by the manufacturer, thereby thwarting low-level malware attacks. Additionally, Windows policies often allow you to define password complexity rules—requiring a minimum length, a mix of characters, or regular password changes. You can also integrate Windows Hello for Business, which adds biometric authentication options. All these measures help maintain the security baseline that is essential for corporate-owned laptops or desktops.

iOS Devices

On Apple's iOS and iPadOS platforms, the focus shifts toward ensuring that the device is not jailbroken, that it uses a passcode, and that it runs a supported version of the operating system. Jailbreaking poses a major security risk because it removes many of the built-in protections Apple provides, opening the device to potentially malicious software. Passcode requirements are important in preventing unauthorized individuals from accessing data, especially when a device is misplaced. You can also enforce specific OS version requirements to make sure that users upgrade to the latest version, which often includes critical security patches. Depending on your organization's needs, you might also require encryption for data at rest, though modern iOS devices typically handle encryption automatically once a passcode is set.

Android Devices

Android is notorious for its fragmentation, with a wide array of manufacturers and versions in circulation. Consequently, compliance settings for Android devices often emphasize OS version requirements to ensure older, vulnerable versions are phased out. You might also enforce disk encryption and mandate specific password rules, such as requiring a strong alphanumeric passcode rather than a simple pattern. Some organizations choose to separate personal and work profiles on Android devices, thereby keeping corporate data in a managed container. This approach is particularly helpful in BYOD scenarios, where employees might hesitate to enroll their entire personal device. By focusing the compliance rules on just the work profile, you protect business apps and data without overreaching into the user's private information.

Despite the differences among platforms, the Intune admin center provides a cohesive experience, so the overall steps are similar across Windows, iOS, and Android. The critical distinction lies in the specific settings you decide to enforce. A well-designed policy takes into account the security capabilities of each platform, as well as the risk profile of your organization. There is no one-size-fits-all strategy; a financial services firm might need more stringent controls than a design agency, for example. Understanding the available settings and aligning them with real-world risk scenarios is key to making sure your compliance policies stay both relevant and manageable.

By following these guidelines, you establish a stable security baseline that applies uniformly across your organization's diverse device landscape. The process of creating compliance policies in Intune might initially appear complex, but once you've defined your essential rules and tested them on pilot devices, the Intune platform automates most of the heavy lifting. Users who meet your criteria gain seamless access to corporate data; those who fail must remedy their devices before proceeding. The result is a living, breathing security ecosystem that continuously checks and reinforces your organization's standards. This dynamic environment not only keeps pace with technological changes but also scales as your company grows, ensuring that even as new devices join the fold, they adhere to the robust guidelines you've put in place.

Assigning and Monitoring Compliance Policies

Creating compliance policies is only the first part of the security puzzle. Once those policies are in place, they need to be distributed to the right devices and continuously monitored. In Intune, the process of assignment connects the rules you have developed with specific device groups or user groups. Monitoring, on the other hand, provides administrators with the real-time visibility they need to make sure every enrolled device meets those standards. While it might sound straightforward—just pick a group and apply a policy—there are several nuances that can help you maintain an organized, efficient environment. By paying attention to how policies are assigned and actively reviewing the resulting data, you ensure that your compliance strategy remains effective rather than turning into a set of static rules that get overlooked.

Assigning Compliance Policies to Device Groups

In Microsoft Intune, administrators can create both device groups and user groups using Azure Active Directory (Azure AD) as the identity backbone. The question of whether to assign policies to a device group or a user group depends on your organization's structure and the specific objectives for each policy. For instance, you might choose device-based targeting when you want all corporate-owned devices to follow certain rules, such as encrypted drives or enforced password complexity. Alternatively, a user-based approach might make more sense if you are securing devices used by employees in a particular department, regardless of whether those devices are corporate-owned or personally owned.

From a strategic perspective, grouping can be as simple or as sophisticated as you wish. Smaller organizations often get by with just a handful of Azure AD groups—one group for Windows devices, one for iOS, and so on. Larger enterprises sometimes build more complex structures, segmenting groups by region, job role, or risk level. Whichever model you adopt, the goal is to map the policies you have created to the groups that actually require them, thereby avoiding unnecessary confusion and potential overlap between multiple sets of rules. Over-assigning the same policy to multiple groups can lead to version control issues and make it harder to troubleshoot. Under-assigning, on the other hand, might leave large swaths of your device landscape without the required security configurations.

When you are ready to assign a policy, you will typically navigate to the Compliance policies section in the Microsoft Endpoint Manager admin center, locate the policy you want to deploy, and then follow a short series of steps that specify which groups it applies to.

1. **Locate the Policy to Assign**
   Begin in the admin center, selecting Devices and then
   Compliance policies. You should see a list of your existing
   policies. Choose the policy that you want to assign, which might
   be labeled something like "Windows 10 – Minimum OS and
   Encryption Policy" or "iOS – Corporate Devices Compliance."

2. **Edit the Policy and Access Assignments**
   Once you select the policy, look for an Assignments option or
   tab, which usually appears on the left navigation panel or near
   the top of the page. Clicking this opens a workspace where you
   can add or remove groups.

3. **Search for the Relevant Group**
   You may type the name of your Azure AD group into a search
   box, or pick from a list of existing groups. The group could be a
   device group if you prefer to target a particular set of hardware,
   or a user group if you want to base compliance on which
   employees are subject to these restrictions.

4. **Confirm and Save**
   After selecting the group, confirm your choice and save the
   changes. Intune then begins the process of applying the policy to
   any devices associated with that group. It might take some time
   for the policy to propagate fully, depending on how many
   devices are within the group and their connectivity.

Completing these steps effectively "ties" the compliance policy to the
group's devices, letting Intune automatically evaluate each device against
the defined security parameters. As devices check in with the Intune
service—which generally happens at various intervals throughout the
day—Intune verifies their configurations, determines whether they
remain compliant, and updates their status accordingly in the admin
center.

Monitoring Compliance Status

Once devices receive these policies, your attention should shift toward monitoring. Monitoring ensures that the environment stays healthy and that any non-compliant devices are quickly identified and remediated. With Intune, you can track compliance status in several ways, the simplest being an at-a-glance summary within the admin center. Typically, the compliance dashboard displays the total number of devices and breaks them down by states such as Compliant, Non-compliant, or In Grace Period. This overview is often enough to give administrators a sense of how the organization is performing overall.

However, beyond this overview lies a treasure trove of details. You might click on the Non-compliant category to see a list of devices that have failed to meet the policy requirements. Each device record will generally show exactly which policy settings it violates—perhaps the device lacks encryption, or the OS is below the required version. If your security model allows for a grace period, you may see some devices listed as being within that window, giving you time to notify users or automatically trigger remediation steps. Meanwhile, devices that repeatedly fail compliance checks might be flagged for immediate action, such as blocking access to corporate email or sensitive applications.

Monitoring often involves more than just reacting to crisis situations. It also lets you identify patterns. For instance, you might realize that many of your iOS devices remain on an outdated OS version because the policy was configured to require the latest release. By spotting this trend early, you can craft a targeted communication plan to remind users to update their devices, explaining the security benefits and providing a simple guide to the upgrade process. Monitoring thus becomes proactive, serving as a feedback loop that helps administrators continuously refine their policies. If a particular requirement proves too difficult for users to meet (for instance, if they have older hardware that doesn't support certain features), you might adjust the policy or develop a new one tailored to that subset of devices.

Generating Reports

Beyond these dashboards and summaries, Intune offers reporting features that allow administrators to create more detailed and often more formal compliance reports. These reports can be invaluable in regulated industries, where auditors might require documented evidence of how data is protected. Even in less regulated environments, they serve as a tangible record of how well your organization complies with its own security standards, enabling you to pinpoint risks and track improvements over time.

There are generally two main ways to generate such reports. The first is using the built-in reporting options within the Microsoft Endpoint Manager admin center. These options usually let you filter by device platform, compliance state, or specific compliance policies. You can quickly export the data to formats like CSV for further analysis in tools like Excel or Power BI. This helps produce visual charts or pivot tables that can highlight patterns, such as spikes in non-compliance after a major OS update or an increase in compliance following a targeted training session.

The second way is to leverage Microsoft Graph APIs, which allow programmatic access to Intune data. Larger enterprises or organizations with custom reporting needs often integrate Intune's compliance data with broader security and analytics platforms. This approach can involve building scheduled scripts or workflows that extract device compliance information on a daily or weekly basis, feed that data into a central data warehouse, and then run sophisticated analytics to cross-reference compliance states with other security signals. While this method is more advanced, it can yield highly customized insights that are particularly useful for complex environments where device compliance is just one piece of a broader puzzle involving network security, identity management, and application monitoring.

Whichever reporting path you choose, the key is to make sure you or your team regularly review the outputs. Having a stack of spreadsheets or a dashboard of metrics doesn't do much good if no one is using it to drive decisions. By establishing a routine—perhaps a weekly check on all non-compliant devices—you can stay ahead of potential issues. If you notice a sudden increase in non-compliance for a particular policy, investigate whether it coincides with a new software patch, a policy change, or even a wave of new devices joining the environment. This continuous loop of setting policies, monitoring compliance, generating reports, and then refining policies is what eventually leads to a mature, resilient security posture.

The Benefits of Consistent Oversight

It's important not to view compliance as a set-and-forget procedure. Even the best policies need regular evaluation, particularly when new device types emerge, operating systems evolve, and employee work habits change. Through careful assignment to the correct device groups, monitoring for anomalies, and generating meaningful reports, organizations can maintain an agile approach. This agility is especially critical in today's digital landscape, where threats evolve rapidly, and a solution that was effective six months ago might now require adjustments. Intune's strength lies not only in providing centralized control but in giving administrators the analytical tools and data they need to remain proactive.

Moreover, a solid monitoring and reporting practice fosters greater transparency and accountability. Employees know what's expected of them and can see the immediate repercussions of ignoring updates or security prompts on their devices. Meanwhile, executives and stakeholders can access clear-cut metrics that prove the organization is actively managing its device fleet. This clarity can be pivotal when communicating with clients, regulators, or business partners who want assurances that their data is well-protected.

Assigning and monitoring compliance policies in Intune is an ongoing cycle rather than a single task. By thoughtfully grouping devices, applying the right policies, and using Intune's extensive monitoring and reporting capabilities, you set the stage for a robust security environment that remains responsive to both organizational goals and the ever-shifting threat landscape. The process can appear simple on the surface—select a group, apply a policy, check a dashboard—but the depth of data and the continuous feedback loop it enables are what truly elevate Intune's device management capabilities. When done properly, this cycle of assignment, monitoring, and reporting transforms compliance from a laborious chore into a powerful strategic asset, reinforcing the broader security posture of your organization.

Real-World Scenario: Implementing Compliance in a Hybrid Environment

The leadership at 365 Strategies had a problem—its employees were scattered across multiple locations, using every type of device imaginable. Some worked full-time in the company's downtown offices, relying on domain-joined laptops that aligned with traditional on-premises security measures. Others split their days between home and client sites, using personally owned tablets or Android phones to review documents and collaborate with colleagues. And a growing number of new hires lived halfway across the country, visiting headquarters only once or twice a year. The company prided itself on flexibility, but that same flexibility invited a host of security concerns. Without a centralized way to enforce compliance and monitor device health, management feared a data breach was inevitable.

As part of its ongoing transformation, 365 Strategies decided to move the majority of its device and application management to Microsoft Intune. Historically, it had used on-premises infrastructure, relying on Group Policy Objects (GPOs) to manage Windows devices. However, GPOs offered limited visibility into the rapidly growing fleet of macOS, iOS, and Android devices, and they did nothing for employees' personal laptops. The IT team led by Chloe Jacobs, the Head of Endpoint Security, realized they needed a more holistic approach. Chloe had read extensively about Intune's capabilities—particularly how it could unify policy enforcement and device compliance checks under one administrative umbrella. Yet she also knew implementing Intune in a hybrid environment, blending cloud management with existing on-premises setups, would be no small feat.

Preparation and Planning

Chloe started by mapping the different device types and user roles within 365 Strategies. The sales department primarily used iPhones and iPads, while the marketing team preferred Android phones. The software development division swore by high-end Windows laptops, and the executive leadership team had a mix of personal Windows and macOS devices. This heterogeneous environment needed a single solution robust enough to handle multiple operating systems but flexible enough to accommodate various user workflows.

Before rolling out Intune company-wide, Chloe decided to launch a pilot program. She selected a cross-section of employees from different departments and asked them to enroll their devices. The pilot was designed to test the new compliance policies the team had drafted, which included mandatory disk encryption for desktops, secure boot for Windows laptops, enforced passcodes on mobile devices, and a minimum operating system version for both mobile and desktop platforms. Chloe configured Intune to link with Azure Active Directory, ensuring that user identities synchronized seamlessly between the on-premises domain and the cloud. This co-management approach allowed the company to keep certain legacy GPO settings temporarily, while Intune took over the more modern compliance requirements.

The pilot uncovered issues almost immediately. Several members of the sales team balked at the idea of enrolling their personal iPhones in what they perceived to be a company-controlled system. Developers complained that certain compliance rules—particularly those requiring immediate OS updates—were disruptive to their workflow, as they often worked with software that required specific Windows versions or dependencies. The IT help desk found itself fielding repeated questions about whether Intune could view personal data or track location. Recognizing these concerns, Chloe held a series of internal Q&A sessions. She explained how Intune's application management segregates corporate apps from personal apps, and that location tracking was disabled in the policies. By the end of the pilot, most employees agreed the benefits of secure access to data outweighed the mild inconveniences of policy enforcement.

Challenges of a Hybrid Deployment

When 365 Strategies moved beyond the pilot phase, the biggest challenge surfaced: reconciling on-premises Windows devices with Intune's cloud management platform. Many of these Windows machines had been joined to the local domain for years, relying on GPOs to handle everything from password policies to software distribution. Shifting those responsibilities to Intune created potential conflicts. For instance, certain GPO settings for Windows Firewall overlapped with Intune's firewall rules, occasionally leaving devices in a state of confusion. Additionally, employees who traveled frequently might not connect to the on-prem network for weeks at a time, making GPO updates sporadic and inconsistent.

Chloe's solution involved carefully auditing existing GPOs and deciding which ones to retire, which to replicate in Intune, and which to keep in place temporarily. She discovered that some old group policies were outdated or irrelevant, left over from a time when employees rarely worked remotely. Meanwhile, others contained essential security components that did not yet exist as Intune policies, requiring custom configuration. By mapping each policy's function, Chloe created a clear transition plan: essential GPO settings would be migrated to Intune equivalents first, while less critical ones would be phased out or rewritten in the weeks to follow.

Another challenge arrived when the IT team realized that a significant number of remote workers were on older Windows versions—some as far back as Windows 8.1—making them incompatible with the newest Intune features. Many of these machines were rarely updated because the employees rarely set foot in the office, so the usual prompts from Windows Update had gone ignored. Deeming these systems non-compliant, Intune restricted them from accessing corporate resources, which in turn led to a surge in support tickets from users suddenly unable to open SharePoint files or Teams chats. Chloe's team had to respond quickly with clear instructions on how to upgrade. Over time, they set up Intune-based enrollment guides and scripts that walked users through the OS upgrade process, ensuring minimal disruption. This situation served as a stark reminder that communication and user enablement are just as critical to a successful security rollout as technology itself.

Integrating Mobility and BYOD

For the mobile segment, one of the biggest hurdles involved reconciling the needs of corporate-owned devices with personal devices. The sales team heavily used iPads for client presentations, but these were purchased and managed by 365 Strategies, so the IT team had full license to enforce restrictions like disabling certain system settings and mandating frequent OS updates. Conversely, employees who used their own Android or iOS phones for quick email checks were understandably resistant to heavier management on personal devices. Chloe worked with her team to craft a set of compliance policies that was less intrusive for BYOD users—focusing mainly on application-level restrictions rather than entire device lockdowns. This approach still required a secure passcode and, if possible, biometric authentication for apps like Outlook. However, it avoided forcing data encryption on the entire device or restricting personal apps, striking a balance that kept the legal department satisfied with data protection measures, while leaving personal content untouched.

To cement these rules, the IT team enabled conditional access in Azure AD, configured to check Intune's compliance status before permitting entry to corporate data. This measure ensured that a user with an outdated operating system or no passcode could not open Teams, SharePoint, or Outlook. The immediate effect was that employees faced a simple choice: either meet the minimal requirements or forego using their devices for work. Most people found it preferable to update their mobile operating systems or set up a fingerprint lock rather than be cut off from their emails and collaborative tools. Over the next few weeks,

Chloe observed a sharp decline in the number of insecure mobile devices accessing the network.

Monitoring, Reporting, and Continual Improvement

As the rollout spread across all departments, 365 Strategies leaned heavily on Intune's compliance dashboard and reporting tools. Chloe made it a point to hold weekly review sessions with her team, checking non-compliant devices and analyzing any emerging patterns. Early in the transition, they noted that a handful of devices repeatedly fell out of compliance each time a new OS update was required. It turned out these users traveled internationally and had limited access to high-speed internet, making them reluctant to download large update files. By contacting these users directly and setting up a local process—sometimes mailing out USB drives containing patch updates—the IT team was able to minimize disruptions and keep those devices secure.

The ongoing reports also proved invaluable whenever the legal or finance departments voiced concerns about data breaches or compliance with industry regulations. With a few clicks, Chloe could generate a report showing how many devices met encryption standards or updated anti-malware definitions. This transparency empowered leadership to make informed decisions, particularly when it came to approving new devices or establishing partnerships with external vendors that required certain security postures.

In parallel, the IT team made small but meaningful improvements to their enrollment instructions and user outreach. For instance, they created a self-service portal where new hires could find step-by-step tutorials on how to enroll devices into Intune. This portal featured screenshots and simple explanations of why each requirement—like disk encryption or a secure lock screen—mattered. Within a few months, the company noticed that new employees adapted far more quickly than those hired before the portal was launched. Enthused by these results, Chloe pushed for ongoing user training that went beyond just compliance. She wanted a culture of security awareness, ensuring employees understood the rationale behind each policy and remained vigilant against threats like phishing or insecure Wi-Fi networks.

Lessons Learned and Looking Ahead

By the end of the first quarter after the Intune deployment, 365 Strategies had made remarkable progress in unifying its disparate device environments. Domain-joined laptops were now co-managed with Intune, maintaining a few legacy GPOs while benefiting from the cloud-based compliance checks. Mobile devices across multiple platforms adhered to a baseline of security policies, with minimal user grumbling once they grasped the need for those requirements. Reports showed a significant decrease in vulnerable OS versions, and remote employees gradually learned to handle updates more proactively. Of course, occasional hiccups occurred—like when a macOS patch broke a third-party design application used by the creative team—but these were dealt with through steady communication, prompt support, and policy adjustments where necessary.

Looking ahead, Chloe and her team plan to phase out most on-premises GPOs entirely, migrating additional policies into Intune. They also intend to experiment with advanced features like risk-based conditional access, which would tie device health signals from Microsoft Defender for Endpoint directly into the compliance engine. If a device shows signs of potential compromise, Intune would immediately mark it as non-compliant, thereby blocking it from critical data until the threat is resolved. For Chloe, this integrated, automated approach represents the pinnacle of endpoint management: a system where compliance policies and real-time threat intelligence work hand in hand to protect corporate resources without micromanaging users.

Although the journey was filled with technical and cultural challenges, 365 Strategies ultimately demonstrated that a hybrid environment need not be a security nightmare. With Intune as the central pillar for compliance, the company found a workable balance between the needs of on-premises infrastructure, remote employees, and bring-your-own-device scenarios. In the process, they reinforced a security-conscious culture that not only met regulatory requirements but also inspired employees to take ownership of protecting corporate data. Through diligent planning, clear communication, and the powerful suite of tools Intune provided, 365 Strategies emerged with a stronger, more adaptive, and more future-proof approach to managing devices in today's complex digital landscape.

Chapter 4: Mastering Conditional Access with Intune

The Basics of Conditional Access

Imagine entering a high-security building where you pass through various checkpoints. At the main entrance, you might show a photo ID and scan a key card to verify you are an authorized individual. Beyond that, certain restricted areas inside the building—like the data center or executive offices—might require an additional biometric scan or a specific passcode. The deeper you go, the more scrutiny you face. This scenario closely mirrors the concept of conditional access in the digital realm. Just as a physical facility implements layered security to protect its most valuable assets, an IT environment uses conditional access to ensure that only trustworthy users and devices can enter sensitive digital spaces.

At its core, conditional access is a policy-based method of regulating user and device access to resources, such as email, documents, or corporate applications. Instead of treating security like a simple on/off switch, conditional access acknowledges the reality that not all logins or connection attempts carry the same level of risk. Consider the difference between a user signing in from a recognized work laptop during regular office hours versus someone trying to access the same data from a foreign country in the middle of the night. The first attempt likely meets a set of expected conditions—trusted device, known geographic location, normal business schedule—while the second raises suspicion and invites a closer look.

Traditionally, networks relied on binary checks that either allowed or denied access based on predefined lists of authorized users. This approach had its place in a simpler world where most work occurred on-site. However, the modern workplace includes a vast range of variables: different device types, constantly shifting user locations, external contractors, and personal devices used for professional tasks.

Conditional access steps in to handle this complexity by examining each user request against multiple factors—such as device health, user credentials, threat intelligence, and more—and then deciding if the request meets the criteria to proceed or should be blocked or challenged.

Microsoft Intune interacts seamlessly with conditional access policies set up in Azure Active Directory (Azure AD). Intune's compliance engine supplies vital information about device health—like whether a device is encrypted or has the latest security updates installed. If Intune finds that a device fails to meet any critical requirements, the device is flagged as non-compliant. Conditional access, in turn, uses that compliance status to determine if the device can reach corporate apps and data. This interdependency creates a real-time feedback loop: if a device falls out of compliance, conditional access can instantly block access to resources until the user resolves the issue. The result is a dynamic defense posture that continually adjusts to evolving threats.

Why Conditional Access Matters

In many ways, conditional access is the linchpin of a zero-trust security model. Zero trust rejects the idea that everything inside a corporate network perimeter can be trusted by default, favoring a stance where every user, device, and app must prove its legitimacy. Just as you wouldn't want anyone who happens to be inside a building to roam freely into the most sensitive rooms, you don't want every device within your network automatically accessing critical data. Conditional access enforces this granular control, ensuring that even if someone has the right username and password, they still face additional checks. This approach greatly limits the damage a leaked password or compromised device can cause.

From an operational standpoint, conditional access also promotes flexibility. It can adapt security requirements based on context rather than applying a one-size-fits-all policy. You might allow single-factor authentication when a user logs in from a known, compliant device on a corporate network, but require multi-factor authentication when that same user tries to log in from an unrecognized device in a different country. This versatility safeguards data without encumbering users with unnecessary steps, thus striking a balance between robust security and a fluid user experience.

Moreover, conditional access integrates well with other Microsoft services and security features. For example, signals from Microsoft Defender for Endpoint about potential malware infections can inform conditional access decisions. If Defender detects a high-risk event on a laptop, that laptop's compliance status might shift, triggering a conditional access policy to block its connection to corporate email or other sensitive apps. This automated interplay reduces the time between detecting a threat and isolating it from critical resources.

Risk-Based Access: A Highway Analogy

To understand risk-based access—one of the most potent features of conditional access—it can help to think of driving on a highway. During typical daylight hours, traffic flows at a standard speed limit. However, if there is a sudden ice storm, the risks of driving at that speed multiply. Consequently, electronic road signs might display lower speed limits, advising drivers to slow down. In some cases, they might even restrict certain lanes or divert traffic altogether if conditions are especially treacherous. The point is that the rules change dynamically in response to shifting risks.

Risk-based conditional access works similarly. Under normal circumstances, a user known to the system, logging in from a location consistent with previous activity, and using a device that meets compliance criteria should have a smooth experience. But if the system identifies abnormal behavior—such as an unexpected geographical login, multiple failed sign-in attempts in a short span, or a high-risk security alert—conditional access can kick in additional requirements or outright deny access. This approach ensures that the security stance adjusts to the situation rather than remaining static.

Several signals feed into risk-based access. One common factor is the user's sign-in risk, gauged by machine learning models that analyze login patterns, IP reputation, and other data points. Another factor is device risk, which draws on compliance information and threat intelligence. Azure AD Identity Protection processes these signals, producing a risk score that conditional access policies then evaluate. If the risk score is low, the user might only need standard credentials. If it's medium, multi-factor authentication might be mandated, or perhaps the user is asked to reset their password. If the risk score is high, access might be blocked altogether. This nimble, context-aware system prevents an attacker with stolen credentials from freely roaming around simply because they guessed or phished someone's password.

The Human Element

While the technology behind conditional access and risk-based access is sophisticated, it's essential not to overlook the human factor. If policies are too strict or confusing, users may become frustrated and seek workarounds. Conversely, if policies are too lenient, the organization is left vulnerable to compromise. Administrators designing conditional access policies must consider the practical implications for everyday workflows. For instance, if employees frequently travel internationally for business, it might not make sense to trigger the highest tier of security checks the moment a login attempt originates outside the country. Instead, you might implement a policy that draws on additional signals, such as whether the device is marked compliant or whether the user is connecting via a known VPN solution.

Likewise, education is key. Employees need to understand what conditional access is and why certain prompts occur. If someone abruptly sees a request for multi-factor authentication at an unusual hour, they might fear it's a glitch or a breach attempt. A brief training session or internal documentation can clarify that risk-based policies sometimes introduce extra security steps based on abnormal conditions. This transparency fosters cooperation rather than resentment, reducing the likelihood that users will circumvent security measures.

Aligning Conditional Access with Business Goals

Conditional access doesn't exist in a vacuum; it must align with broader business objectives and regulatory requirements. Many organizations operate under compliance mandates like HIPAA, GDPR, or PCI-DSS, each imposing various rules on data protection. Conditional access helps to enforce these mandates by ensuring that only approved devices and users access sensitive information. For instance, a hospital might set a policy that any device accessing patient records must be encrypted and located within a certain network range. The moment a device fails to meet these criteria—say, an employee tries to open patient data on an unencrypted personal phone at home—conditional access can automatically block that access. This capability not only fortifies security but also simplifies audits, as administrators can produce evidence that the system denies non-compliant connections by design.

On the business side, conditional access can support new initiatives like bring-your-own-device (BYOD) programs or flexible remote working options. Instead of issuing a hard "no" to personal devices or remote connections, organizations can institute a more nuanced policy that allows them—provided the device and user meet compliance checks. This encourages innovation and employee satisfaction, as workers can use the tools and schedules that best suit their productivity, without opening the organization to undue risk.

Monitoring and Evolving Policies

An essential aspect of conditional access is that it's not a set-and-forget mechanism. Because threats evolve and business needs change, administrators should regularly review policy performance. Azure AD and Intune dashboards provide insights into which policies trigger the most frequently, how often users face sign-in challenges, and whether certain risk signals appear repeatedly. Reviewing these data points helps you decide if a particular policy is too aggressive or too lax.

For instance, you might notice that every Monday morning after a major OS update, a spike in devices is temporarily flagged as non-compliant. This pattern could indicate that your enforcement window is too narrow, or that you need clearer communications encouraging users to update their devices over the weekend. Conversely, if you never see any high-risk sign-in events, it could be that your environment is unusually secure—or that your policies aren't stringent enough to catch suspicious behavior. By periodically evaluating these metrics, you can refine your conditional access setup to reflect the current threat landscape and user behavior.

Building a Culture of Conditional Thinking

Ultimately, conditional access represents a mindset shift in security management—a move from static rules to dynamic, context-aware controls. Rather than trusting every device that crosses the firewall, the system continuously evaluates whether conditions meet specific standards. Instead of allowing a user endless access once they've typed a password, the system reevaluates risk based on location, device health, and user behavior. Organizations that embrace this approach typically find they can maintain higher security standards without imposing blanket restrictions on every scenario. Employees appreciate the minimized friction when working in low-risk situations, while the organization gains confidence that unusual or suspicious activities won't go unchecked.

By weaving together identity checks, device compliance, and real-time risk analysis, conditional access adds a powerful layer to modern cybersecurity. As you proceed through this chapter, you will discover how to create and fine-tune these policies in Intune and Azure AD, how to incorporate advanced signals like threat intelligence, and how to ensure that the user experience remains manageable. This shift to a contextual, adaptive model isn't just about meeting today's security demands—it sets the foundation for a future in which organizations can respond promptly and decisively to threats that evolve by the hour. Much like a high-security building with layered checkpoints, your digital environment becomes a place where trust must be earned continuously, thereby safeguarding your most valuable resources in an ever-changing world.

Configuring Conditional Access Policies in Azure AD and Intune

Once you understand the principles behind conditional access—namely, that it evaluates each login attempt against contextual signals and device compliance—you can begin setting up these policies in Azure Active Directory (Azure AD). For most administrators, this involves several phases: planning which conditions warrant additional scrutiny, deciding who or what is in scope, and then integrating Microsoft Intune so that device health status directly informs the access decision. Although the process might appear daunting at first, Azure AD's interface simplifies the creation of policies by breaking the workflow into understandable segments. By the end of this configuration journey, you should have a dynamic mechanism that either grants, challenges, or denies access based on real-time risk factors.

Foundations of Conditional Access Configuration

Before diving into the technical steps, it helps to reaffirm the overarching purpose of conditional access. It is not merely a blanket solution that blocks or allows everything. Instead, it applies specific checks depending on the situation. For instance, a user logging into Office 365 from a compliant, corporate-issued laptop might face minimal friction, whereas a user connecting from an unpatched device in an unfamiliar country may be prompted for multi-factor authentication or blocked outright. Azure AD's conditional access framework offers a wide range of "conditions" you can define—such as device platform, sign-in risk level, IP location, and more—and couples them with "controls," which outline what should happen when those conditions are met.

Meanwhile, Microsoft Intune performs device compliance checks, ensuring that devices adhere to security baselines like encryption, minimum OS versions, and password complexity. Once a device is deemed compliant, that status is relayed back to Azure AD. This interplay means your conditional access policy can include a rule such as "Require device to be marked as compliant," effectively shutting out any device that doesn't meet the specified criteria. By merging these capabilities, your environment transitions from a static, one-size-fits-all security posture to a dynamic, risk-responsive system.

Getting Started in Azure AD

To configure a new conditional access policy, you typically begin in the Azure AD admin center. If you are also managing Intune, you may access the same environment via the Microsoft Endpoint Manager admin center and navigate to the security settings. Regardless of your starting point, the experience converges on Azure AD's Security blade, which contains the Conditional Access option. Here, you can view existing policies or create a new one. Each policy you create walks you through a similar pattern:

1. **Naming and Description**: You start by giving your policy a name that indicates its purpose. For instance, a policy might be called "Enforce Compliance for Office 365" if its goal is to ensure only compliant devices can access core productivity apps. A concise description helps clarify its intent for other administrators or future reference.

2. **Assigning Users or Groups**: The next step is determining which individuals or groups the policy should apply to. Some policies might be broader, targeting all employees and contractors in the tenant. Others could be narrower, applying only to executives or to a specific team that handles sensitive financial data. You can also exclude certain user groups if needed. This granular assignment model helps tailor the strength of your security measures to the actual risk level of each role.

3. **Selecting Cloud Apps or Actions**: Conditional access can limit or grant access to specific apps in your Microsoft 365 environment, including Exchange Online, SharePoint, Teams, or even third-party SaaS applications that integrate with Azure AD. If, for example, you want to protect mailbox data in Exchange Online, you select that app in the policy so it's governed by your chosen conditions. You also have an option to protect "All cloud

apps," which is a more sweeping approach but may be appropriate for organizations that want a consistent security baseline everywhere.

4. **Defining Conditions**: This is where you specify triggers such as sign-in risk, device platform, location, or client apps. For instance, you might choose to apply stricter rules if users try to sign in from an IP address not recognized on your trusted list or from a certain geographic region prone to cyber threats. You can also look at the type of device platform—Windows, iOS, Android, or macOS—and impose different rules accordingly. If your organization leverages Azure AD Identity Protection, you can incorporate user risk or sign-in risk levels into these conditions, further refining who gets challenged or blocked under specific circumstances.

5. **Configuring Access Controls**: After specifying the conditions, you move on to the controls—what should happen if those conditions are met. For instance, you might require multi-factor authentication (MFA), block legacy authentication methods, or mandate that the device be marked as compliant by Intune. The latter is where Intune truly shines in a conditional access scenario. By selecting "Require device to be marked as compliant," you ensure that any device flagged as non-compliant cannot proceed, effectively preventing access for devices that fail your established security baselines.

6. **Enforcement and Reporting**: Finally, before saving the policy, Azure AD prompts you to decide whether to enable it immediately. Some administrators opt for a "Report-only" mode or a phased rollout to avoid inadvertently locking out large numbers of users. Once enabled, any sign-in attempt meeting the conditions triggers the controls you've designated, and Azure AD logs those events for your review. This logging aspect is crucial for ongoing management and helps you fine-tune policies based on real-world outcomes.

Integrating Intune Policies

As soon as you enable the "Require device to be marked as compliant" control, Azure AD begins relying on Intune's compliance engine to provide a real-time assessment of each device. This connection is already established when you enroll devices in Intune and link your device management tenant to Azure AD. In practical terms, whenever a user initiates a sign-in to a protected app or service, Azure AD queries the device's compliance status. If the device meets all the criteria—such as running the minimum OS version and having disk encryption turned on—Intune marks it compliant. Azure AD then checks your conditional access policy to confirm that compliance is required, sees that the condition is satisfied, and grants access.

If a device is out of compliance, Azure AD references your policy's configuration to determine the outcome. Often, administrators block non-compliant devices outright. However, you might choose a softer approach, such as triggering a "remediation" workflow: sending an email or push notification telling the user how to fix the issue. This strategy aims to guide employees back into compliance rather than instantly denying their ability to work. Intune can also display messages through its Company Portal app (on mobile devices) or through other device-based notifications, instructing users to update their OS or enable encryption. The policy's logic then rechecks the device periodically or after each sign-in attempt, granting or denying access based on whether the problem has been addressed.

Handling Exceptions and Complex Use Cases

Inevitably, some situations demand a nuanced approach. For example, what about devices used by external consultants who cannot fully comply with your internal policies? Or specialized hardware running legacy operating systems for which encryption is not practical? Azure AD's conditional access policies let you carve out exceptions by excluding certain user groups or configuring additional logic. You might create a "Contractor Exceptions" group that is allowed access to basic apps but blocked from the most sensitive data. Alternatively, you could rely on a risk-based strategy that challenges these devices with multifactor prompts more frequently, striking a balance between convenience and security.

Another complex scenario involves shared devices, such as kiosks or point-of-sale terminals. Because these devices typically do not tie to a single user identity, they can be tricky to manage from a compliance standpoint. One approach is to set up a specialized compliance policy in Intune that accounts for the device's unique function—enforcing only essential settings like mandatory password protection or restricted user privileges. Then, you tailor the conditional access policy to accept that specialized compliance state. This ensures employees can still perform kiosk-related tasks without giving them unfettered access to corporate email or sensitive documents.

Continuous Monitoring and Adaptation

Creating a policy is just the beginning. After you enable it, the real work involves monitoring its impact. Azure AD's Sign-in logs and Intune's device compliance reports both furnish insight into how often users are blocked or challenged, which devices fail compliance checks most frequently, and whether suspicious activities go unchecked. You might discover that a large chunk of your mobile workforce regularly hits the policy's friction points—perhaps they are traveling in locations you flagged as high-risk. Armed with these logs, you can choose to refine the conditions to avoid unnecessary inconvenience or strengthen them further if you see real threats.

In some cases, monitoring data reveals that certain controls are too lax. If a high percentage of attempted hacks originate from one or two IP addresses that keep trying to authenticate, you might want to block sign-ins from that region altogether. Conversely, you could decide that multi-factor authentication is required for all external connections, not just high-risk ones. This kind of iterative policy tuning transforms conditional access from a static rule set into a living defense mechanism that evolves in response to your organization's changing needs and threat landscape.

A Cornerstone of Modern Security

The synergy between Azure AD conditional access and Intune's compliance policies lies at the heart of a comprehensive, forward-looking security strategy. Together, they provide the levers for controlling who, what, when, and where your sensitive data can be accessed. In a world where employees log in from personal tablets on public Wi-Fi, where contractors occasionally need limited network privileges, and where advanced threats aim to exploit every gap, conditional access fills the role of a vigilant gatekeeper. It scrutinizes each request, consults real-time data on device compliance, and then decides which privileges to grant or withhold—all without bringing legitimate business operations to a standstill.

For many organizations, the initial challenge is shifting the mindset from traditional on-premises controls and simple password-based logins to a cloud-first, contextual approach. Yet once administrators see how Azure AD and Intune integrate to enforce consistent rules across varied devices, the value becomes apparent. Instead of chasing down each potential vulnerability or running frantic manual audits, your system does the heavy lifting. Every sign-in is a chance to confirm whether a device, user, and context meet the criteria you've deemed acceptable. This not only raises your security baseline but also delivers a scalable framework that can adapt to new applications, new device types, or even new business models as your company grows.

Configuring conditional access policies in Azure AD and leveraging Intune for device compliance is less about checking boxes and more about embracing a dynamic, modern approach to cybersecurity. By combining the granular controls of Azure AD with the robust endpoint checks of Intune, you create a layered defense that accounts for all the nuances of real-world work scenarios. Whether you're a global enterprise managing thousands of devices or a smaller organization looking to safeguard sensitive client data, this partnership between identity protection and endpoint compliance stands as one of the most effective strategies to maintain security in today's cloud-focused, zero-trust era.

Case Study: Protecting Data with Conditional Access

When 365 Strategies first embarked on its journey to modernize IT, the leadership team knew one goal stood above all others: protect company data without hindering employees' ability to innovate and collaborate. The organization had a global footprint, with offices in North America, Europe, and parts of Asia. This geographic spread was an asset for working with international clients, but it also introduced complexities in how employees accessed key systems. Some worked primarily in an office environment, while others traveled incessantly, connecting from cafés, hotels, or home networks. A smaller yet significant percentage of the workforce was fully remote, often using personal devices to log in. Ensuring that each of these varied setups maintained robust security standards seemed daunting.

The company had a few hodgepodge tools in place—virtual private networks (VPNs) for remote access, separate mobile device management (MDM) for smartphones, and on-premises Active Directory policies for older Windows laptops. But these tools worked in isolation, offering no central visibility or consistent enforcement. Attempting to track the security posture of devices across continents became a massive undertaking for the IT security group. The final straw came when the organization discovered that a remote worker's laptop, missing several months' worth of crucial patches, had been compromised by a known vulnerability. Fortunately, the data breach was contained before it escalated, but the incident set alarm bells ringing. Clearly, 365 Strategies needed a unified solution.

Identifying the Gaps

The first step was a comprehensive audit. Under the guidance of IT Director Alex Wu, the company hired an external consultancy to assess its security posture. The consultants found a handful of glaring issues. Foremost among them was that employees used various devices, each running different operating system versions and lacking uniform security settings. Some laptops adhered to password policies from on-premises Group Policy Objects (GPOs), while smartphones and tablets operated with minimal oversight. Cloud services—particularly for file sharing—exposed even more vulnerabilities, since many employees simply used a single sign-on password without further checks. Additionally, some staff members bypassed official channels altogether, saving sensitive documents to personal file-hosting platforms for easy access on the go. While leadership valued this kind of flexibility, they realized it posed a substantial risk in a world of escalating cyber threats.

After gathering all these insights, Alex convened a meeting with the executive committee to propose an overhaul of the organization's security architecture. His solution hinged on the adoption of Microsoft Intune for device compliance and Azure Active Directory's conditional access. This integrated approach promised to unify every type of device under a single policy framework, automatically adapting to the context and risk level of each login attempt. Although the executive team had concerns—particularly around user adoption and the possibility of over-restricting legitimate work—they gave Alex the green light, recognizing that the alternative was continuing to gamble with data security.

Laying the Groundwork

Alex and his team embarked on the preliminary work of enrolling devices into Intune, which allowed them to define baseline compliance policies. One policy demanded that all Windows laptops, whether corporate-owned or BYOD, run the latest feature update within three months of release. Another required that mobile devices set up for business email have a secure passcode and a minimum operating system version. The team also introduced an encryption requirement for macOS machines. In parallel, they created a dedicated communication channel to brief employees on why these changes were necessary. They explained that while this move might require small adjustments, such as a mandatory OS update or a more complex passcode, it was ultimately about protecting the entire organization's data and reputation.

Still, the puzzle wasn't complete until the team set up conditional access policies in Azure Active Directory. Their plan was to tackle the highest-value resources first: email, document repositories, and the financial applications used for invoicing and budgeting. The idea was simple but potent: whenever a user tried to access these resources, Azure AD would check whether the device was marked as compliant by Intune. If not, the user would be blocked or prompted to address the non-compliance before proceeding.

The architecture also incorporated risk-based rules. Alex knew that some employees, especially in sales and consulting, had unpredictable travel schedules. They might log in from an airport lounge in Tokyo one day and a hotel in London the next. In the past, each new location triggered a flood of help-desk tickets, as the system might block them purely based on geographic filtering. With conditional access, the plan was more nuanced. Rather than always denying foreign IP addresses, the system would weigh several factors: the sign-in risk rating derived by Azure AD Identity Protection, the user's device compliance status, and whether the device had a legitimate, up-to-date antivirus solution. If everything checked out, the user would only face a mild prompt, such as multi-factor authentication (MFA). If the system saw suspicious signals—like multiple failed login attempts in a short span or indications of malware infection—access would be denied outright.

Rolling Out Policies and Adjusting in Real Time

The rollout began in a phased manner, targeting one department at a time. The finance team, who regularly handled sensitive financial data, was first. By focusing on them, Alex could calibrate the policies in an environment where stakes were high and employee numbers were relatively small. Initially, about a quarter of finance staff found themselves blocked due to non-compliant devices—mostly personal laptops that had never been fully patched or phones that lacked device passcodes. The block messages explained why they were denied and offered instructions on how to rectify the issue. Although some employees grumbled about losing immediate access, most recognized the necessity once they understood the potential risks of an unsecured device. Within a week, nearly all finance staff had remediated their devices, and the number of blocked access attempts dropped dramatically.

The next test came when the marketing department was brought under the conditional access umbrella. Unlike finance, marketing had a high mix of BYOD usage, with employees frequently working off personal Macs or Android phones. A significant portion of them also worked flexible hours, sometimes uploading event photos or promotional materials at odd times. To accommodate their workflow, the IT team allowed some exceptions—employees could continue using older macOS versions for a short grace period if they had documented software compatibility issues, provided they took other security measures like enabling disk encryption. Alex and the team learned the value of building a feedback loop: each time a user encountered a stumbling block, the help desk documented it, identified the root cause, and passed that information to the security architects to see if the policy needed refinement. This iterative process smoothed out the initial friction and gave marketing staff a sense of ownership in shaping the new system.

Observing Tangible Results

Shortly after marketing fully adopted the new policies, an event occurred that showcased the real power of conditional access. An employee named Priya attempted to log in to the company's SharePoint site from a hotel Wi-Fi network in a high-risk region. Azure AD flagged suspicious behavior: several rapid login attempts had come from a different part of the world earlier that same day on the same user account. This discrepancy triggered a higher-than-usual risk score. Conditional access automatically demanded multi-factor authentication. Priya, who was legitimately at the hotel, passed the prompt with her authenticator app. Meanwhile, the suspicious login attempts—now recognized as unauthorized—were thwarted, unable to bypass the MFA layer. When the security team investigated, they found that someone had tried to brute-force Priya's password. Without the additional conditional access checks, that attacker might have slipped into the system unnoticed if they eventually guessed the password. This incident highlighted how combining device compliance and location risk analysis could neutralize threats in real time.

Beyond such near-misses, 365 Strategies gathered tangible data demonstrating that employees were updating and patching their devices more consistently. Intune's reporting made it easy for department heads to see who was in or out of compliance, turning it into a team-oriented effort rather than a purely top-down directive. The help desk also observed fewer calls related to security blocks over time, as users acclimated to the new requirements. In the first month, there had been a spike in "access denied" queries, but within three months, those queries diminished to a trickle. For the leadership team, this consistent compliance represented a major leap forward, both for security and for potential audits tied to industry regulations.

Lessons Learned

In retrospect, Alex and his colleagues identified a few critical lessons that might help other organizations on a similar path. The first was the importance of user education. Simply enabling policies without explaining the "why" behind them would have produced a backlash of confusion and frustration. By hosting informational sessions, providing FAQ documents, and directly addressing concerns about privacy and device ownership, 365 Strategies forged a sense of partnership with employees. People were more willing to comply when they saw how easy it was to meet the new requirements, and how those requirements protected them from phishing attacks or potential data theft.

The second lesson was that iterative policy refinement is crucial. The security team avoided rolling out a single, perfect policy for the entire company at once. Instead, they experimented with smaller groups, solicited feedback, monitored logs, and made incremental tweaks. This agility helped them tailor conditional access to the unique needs of each department—finance, marketing, software development, and so on— without sacrificing the overarching security goals.

Third, they discovered how much simpler auditing and reporting became once Intune and Azure AD formed the backbone of their security model. Instead of juggling half a dozen different tools, the IT team had a central dashboard to view device compliance, risk events, and user activity. This consolidation not only saved time but also provided a clearer snapshot of the company's overall security posture. In regulated contexts, these clear dashboards and exportable logs were invaluable during compliance checks, as they could quickly show which devices had full encryption and which users were following multi-factor authentication protocols.

Finally, the experience underscored that conditional access is not a static project with a fixed end date, but rather an evolving strategy. 365 Strategies planned to integrate additional signals, such as real-time threat intelligence from Microsoft Defender for Endpoint, into their conditional access flow. This way, if a device displayed signs of compromise—like evidence of malware or abnormal network traffic—conditional access could immediately block its attempt to access sensitive applications until security teams resolved the issue. Such integrations would extend the protective umbrella, ensuring that each device not only passed the standard compliance checks but also wasn't actively under attack.

365 Strategies' journey highlights the transformative power of combining Intune's device compliance capabilities with Azure AD conditional access. By addressing employees' fears, refining policies through iterative feedback, and centralizing reporting, the organization cultivated a security culture where risk evaluation and data protection coexisted with the flexibility workers craved. The outcome was a more resilient environment where threats were detected, challenged, and blocked long before they compromised critical data. And, perhaps more importantly, it was an environment where security felt like a shared responsibility rather than an imposition—a goal that any organization, regardless of size or sector, can aspire to achieve.

Chapter 5: Advanced Compliance and Access Control Strategies

Integrating Intune with Other Microsoft Security Tools

The modern security landscape is a tapestry of interwoven components, each designed to address a specific layer of risk. Even though Microsoft Intune excels at managing device compliance and configuring access policies, it truly shines when integrated with other security tools to form a cohesive defense strategy. Among these tools, Microsoft Defender for Endpoint stands out as a natural partner. Formerly known by various names like Windows Defender ATP, Microsoft Defender for Endpoint has evolved into a cloud-powered service that delivers endpoint detection and response (EDR), advanced threat intelligence, and real-time remediation features. When Intune and Defender for Endpoint work in unison, organizations gain a unified view of each device's posture, combining compliance data with live threat intelligence. This integration underscores the power of a comprehensive security approach, allowing teams to respond swiftly to threats while maintaining the high-level governance required in increasingly regulated industries.

The Rationale for a Unified Defense

To understand why unifying security tools around Intune and Defender for Endpoint is so beneficial, it helps to revisit the concept of zero-trust security. In a zero-trust model, each connection attempt—whether from a user, device, or application—requires verification. Credentials alone are insufficient; the device's health, risk signals, and context must also prove trustworthy. While Intune can enforce device-level compliance checks (like requiring encryption or up-to-date operating systems), it does not inherently recognize threats such as active malware infections or suspicious network behavior. That's where Defender for Endpoint steps in, acting as a real-time sentinel that scans for unusual processes, malicious executables, and other indicators of compromise.

By feeding that information back into Intune, an organization gains the ability to automatically alter a device's compliance status if new threats emerge. For example, if Defender for Endpoint detects a high-severity alert on a laptop—perhaps indicating that ransomware was detected—Intune can promptly mark that device as non-compliant. This status then flows into Azure Active Directory's conditional access engine, blocking or restricting the device's access to critical corporate data until the security issue is resolved. The result is a closed-loop system: discover threats, quarantine or remediate them, and prevent the device from posing an organizational risk during that window of vulnerability.

Setting Up Integration with Defender for Endpoint

For administrators seeking to tie Intune and Defender for Endpoint together, the process typically involves configuring a tenant-level connector in the Microsoft Endpoint Manager admin center. A few steps—such as enabling the Microsoft Defender for Endpoint integration, creating a device compliance policy that references Defender's risk level, and syncing device inventory—are required to establish communication between the two services. Once connected, each device in Intune can be seen in the Defender for Endpoint portal as well, along with aggregated threat details. Additionally, administrators can enable features such as automated investigation and response (AIR), which helps detect, analyze, and, in some scenarios, automatically neutralize threats.

These integrations unfold at different depths based on an organization's licensing and security maturity. Some prefer minimal connections, allowing Defender for Endpoint primarily to collect and analyze threat signals in the background. Others opt for a more aggressive posture, turning on real-time enforcement so that any device flagged as "high risk" is immediately blocked from accessing corporate resources via conditional access policies. This approach suits environments where data sensitivity is extremely high, or where threat actors regularly target endpoints in sophisticated ways. Ultimately, the goal is to blend the device-centric compliance model of Intune with the advanced, intelligence-driven detection in Defender for Endpoint, creating a synergy that surpasses what either solution could achieve alone.

The Broader Microsoft Ecosystem

Of course, Defender for Endpoint is only one part of Microsoft's security ecosystem. Solutions like Microsoft Defender for Cloud Apps (formerly MCAS) provide visibility into SaaS applications, enabling organizations to identify shadow IT or risky user behaviors in the cloud. Additionally, Microsoft Sentinel—a cloud-native SIEM (Security Information and Event Management) and SOAR (Security Orchestration, Automation, and Response) platform—collects logs and alerts from across the Microsoft stack and beyond, correlating events to pinpoint threats that might otherwise remain hidden. When each piece of the puzzle shares data with Intune, administrators gain an extensive, unified perspective on security.

For instance, you could configure Sentinel to receive alerts whenever Defender for Endpoint flags a high-risk event. Sentinel could then correlate these alerts with user sign-in anomalies logged by Azure AD. If it detects a pattern—like repeated suspicious sign-ins from unknown IPs combined with endpoint malware warnings—it can automatically enrich the alert and notify the security team. Meanwhile, Intune, already aware that Defender for Endpoint deemed the device high risk, escalates the compliance status accordingly, and conditional access locks down that device's privileges until a resolution is confirmed. This orchestrated approach shortens the gap between threat detection and response. In some cases, it might even automate parts of the investigation, freeing security analysts to focus on higher-level strategizing rather than manual containment tasks.

Unified Security, Tangible Benefits

An important advantage of weaving Intune into a holistic security environment is that employees often have fewer standalone apps or dashboards to manage. Rather than juggling separate security agents, patching tools, and endpoint protection programs, they interact primarily with the tools they already know—like Windows security settings, the

Company Portal app on mobile, or integrated dashboards in Microsoft 365. Meanwhile, the various back-end services (Intune, Defender, Azure AD, Sentinel) coordinate to apply consistent policies across an organization's entire device landscape. This reduces user confusion and fosters better adherence to policies, since employees can take advantage of streamlined enrollment and threat notifications.

Similarly, IT departments benefit from unified reporting and analytics. With Intune feeding device compliance data to Defender for Endpoint, and vice versa, generating executive-level reports on overall endpoint health becomes far simpler. Decision-makers can see how many devices are currently flagged as high-risk or how many attacks have been averted within a specific window. They can even measure how quickly the organization remediates threats. Such metrics can be invaluable for demonstrating compliance with regulations or justifying further investment in cybersecurity. And because all the data resides within the Microsoft cloud ecosystem, there's a lower risk of data fragmentation or incomplete threat intelligence.

Another subtle yet vital benefit is simpler licensing and support overhead. While it's true that different Microsoft 365 or Enterprise Mobility + Security (EMS) plans provide varying levels of Defender for Endpoint capabilities, having a single vendor manage the entire stack can streamline contract renewals, version upgrades, and troubleshooting. If an issue arises between Intune and Defender for Endpoint, you have one main point of contact in Microsoft support, rather than juggling multiple support providers who might pass you back and forth.

A Real-World Example

To see these principles in action, consider 365 Strategies, which had been relying heavily on Intune for device compliance and conditional access. As the company expanded, leadership recognized that reactive security measures were no longer sufficient. They had minimal insight into advanced threats targeting endpoints, especially since the workforce included remote employees and contractors using a mix of Windows, macOS, Android, and iOS devices. After implementing Microsoft

Defender for Endpoint, the security team configured Intune policies to treat "high-risk" devices—those flagged by Defender for Endpoint's analytics—as non-compliant.

Within weeks of going live, an overseas contractor's laptop was compromised by a sophisticated keylogging tool, which Defender for Endpoint swiftly detected. The system flagged the device as high risk, triggering Intune to mark it as non-compliant. Conditional access then denied the contractor's attempts to access the company's SharePoint portal. This automated response likely prevented a major data breach. The security team then used Defender's forensic tools to investigate the scope of the infection. Armed with a timeline of the malware's behavior, they worked with the contractor to rebuild the laptop, re-enroll it in Intune, and confirm the absence of any lingering threats. Throughout the entire process, the only immediate business impact was that the compromised device could not reach sensitive data; other employees worked uninterrupted, thanks to the granular nature of conditional access policies.

Paving the Way for Future Innovations

As Microsoft continues to evolve its security lineup, the Intune-Defender integration will only grow more sophisticated. Already, organizations can enable features like endpoint vulnerability assessment, which scans for missing patches or misconfigurations, then relays those vulnerabilities back to Intune for potential remediation. Future advancements might include deeper AI-driven threat hunting, cross-platform coverage for Linux and IoT devices, and even more refined risk-based policies that adapt to each endpoint's context in real time. By integrating Intune with the broader Microsoft security ecosystem, organizations essentially future-proof their security strategy, ensuring they can tap into new developments without a major architectural overhaul.

Of course, success depends on more than just turning on a connector. As with any advanced security implementation, planning and governance are crucial. Organizations must define clear policies that specify how device risk is determined, which actions should be taken at each risk level, and who is responsible for handling escalations. Training the help desk team to interpret Defender for Endpoint alerts—or at least direct them to the right security analysts—can prevent minor incidents from spiraling into more significant problems. Likewise, if a "zero-tolerance" approach to high-risk devices is implemented, you'll want to educate employees on what steps they need to take to regain access if their device is quarantined. When everyone understands the rationale and the mechanics of the process, compliance feels less like a burden and more like a shared responsibility for safeguarding organizational assets.

A Holistic Shield

In the ever-evolving tapestry of modern cyber threats, no single tool or policy can offer complete protection. Security is, by nature, a layered discipline that aims to minimize risk at every stage. By integrating Intune with Microsoft Defender for Endpoint, organizations gain a powerful synergy. Intune's device compliance ensures a baseline of security hygiene—like updated operating systems and encryption—while Defender's threat intelligence and real-time alerts catch active attacks in progress. When one sees a problem, the other responds. This level of orchestration closes the gap between threat detection and remediation, turning a crisis into a manageable incident that can be swiftly contained.

Furthermore, a unified approach extends beyond just Intune and Defender for Endpoint. Solutions like Azure AD conditional access, Microsoft Sentinel, and Microsoft 365 security features can all plug into the same hub of shared data and signals. The cohesive view helps administrators identify suspicious patterns that might span multiple tools, and it gives leadership a single pane of glass for evaluating the overall security posture. Most importantly, an environment managed holistically is one that encourages best practices across the board— employees face consistent policies, devices receive uniform monitoring, and threat data flows freely among the services best equipped to act on it.

In essence, unifying Intune with other Microsoft security tools transforms a patchwork of protective measures into a seamless defense mechanism. It is an approach that fosters agility in addressing threats, clarity in policymaking, and confidence that devices remain compliant both now and in the future. For organizations large and small, this synergy is quickly becoming the new standard for modern endpoint security—and a foundational step toward truly zero-trust operations.

Customizing Policies for Different User Groups

In many organizations, a single compliance or access control policy rarely suffices for every role. Consider the variety of responsibilities and risk profiles within a typical enterprise: executives who handle sensitive financial data, a marketing team that needs flexible device usage, and contract workers who only require short-term access to select systems. If each of these groups were restricted by an identical set of rules, inefficiencies would abound. High-level users might be overburdened by strict controls that impair collaboration, or employees with minimal data access could be subject to unnecessary security layers. The real power of Microsoft Intune, especially in tandem with other Microsoft security services, lies in creating custom policies aligned with both an organization's risk tolerance and the demands of each user population.

Recognizing the Need for Segmentation

Before diving into policy creation, it helps to understand why segmentation matters. At its core, segmentation is about aligning security with business realities. This means creating policy sets that reflect the distinct roles or departments within your company, their specific operational needs, and the sensitivity of the data they handle. By drawing these lines, you can apply more robust controls where the stakes are highest, while maintaining more flexible guidelines in areas that pose a lower risk. Such stratification not only elevates overall security but also increases user satisfaction, as employees are less likely to grapple with rules that are irrelevant or excessively strict for their specific jobs.

To achieve this, administrators often map out a matrix that includes user roles, device ownership models (corporate-owned versus personal), geographic locations, and even usage patterns. From there, they can establish targeted security baselines. For example, a traveling salesperson frequently working in high-risk regions may face more stringent access controls than an internal IT specialist who logs in solely from the company's network. This customization is doubly important when your workforce is large or global, encompassing multiple cultures, compliance obligations, or device preferences. Intune provides the building blocks for such segmentation by allowing administrators to create Azure Active Directory (Azure AD) groups and nest policies specifically for each scenario.

Tailoring by Role

Role-based customization is perhaps the most common approach. You begin by identifying user groups—executives, finance, human resources, marketing, sales, IT, contractors—and delineating their responsibilities and data access needs. Each group often requires a different blend of Intune settings and compliance checks. An executive group, for instance, could be subject to stricter rules for device encryption and multi-factor authentication (MFA), given the potentially sensitive data they handle, such as corporate strategy, merger details, or confidential partner agreements. Meanwhile, marketing staff, who frequently work with large multimedia files, might benefit from less aggressive enforcement of certain encryption standards if their tasks involve collaborative design software that occasionally clashes with encryption protocols. The marketing group could instead rely on a streamlined set of compliance rules—like ensuring a modern operating system and a strong passcode— without restricting the variety of devices they use.

As an example, consider 365 Strategies, where the finance department deals with sensitive client billing information. The IT team sets up a compliance policy that mandates disk encryption for any finance-related device, alongside a minimum OS version to ensure the presence of the most recent security patches. Additionally, the policy enforces multi-factor authentication for every login attempt, reflecting the heightened risk of credential theft in financial contexts. Conversely, the creative design team is still required to adhere to basic compliance—like an up-to-date operating system and enforced password complexity—yet is afforded more leeway regarding software installations. The outcome is a balanced environment: finance users follow robust measures that address critical data risks, while creative staff maintain enough flexibility to meet project deadlines without wading through unnecessary security obstacles.

Location-Based Policies

Location-based policies introduce another layer of granularity. Not all offices or access points offer the same level of security. On-campus networks, for instance, tend to be more trusted, protected by firewalls, intrusion detection systems, and regular monitoring. Remote or public networks, such as those found in cafés or coworking spaces, pose a higher risk. In a location-based scheme, Intune can tap into Azure AD conditional access to determine whether users are connecting from "trusted locations" (e.g., headquarters or known branch offices) or "untrusted locations" (public Wi-Fi, international networks, or unknown IP addresses). Depending on the context, you can apply different rules or require extra forms of authentication.

In practice, this might mean that employees in the office can open basic corporate resources on a compliant device without repeatedly prompting for MFA. However, if they attempt to access the same resources from an unrecognized IP range, the system will demand additional verification. For organizations that have traveling employees who require consistent access, location-based policies might allow them to request a short-term exception by registering their IP address or network as semi-trusted during the length of their stay. If corporate security posture is conservative, the system might block all logins from high-risk locations entirely, or at least enforce advanced security measures such as mandatory VPN usage or continuous monitoring.

Some companies even enforce geolocation policies to prevent data access from certain high-risk or sanctioned countries. In such cases, Azure AD sees the originating IP location and either denies sign-in attempts outright or prompts the user with extra security challenges. Since Intune tracks device compliance data as well, the system can decide that connecting from an untrusted location is permissible only if the device meets specific requirements—for example, an up-to-date antivirus engine or a specified patch level. This synergy provides a high degree of control while still respecting legitimate work-from-anywhere scenarios.

Risk-Level Adjustments

Modern security strategies often hinge on a risk-based approach, continuously evaluating user behavior and device health to detect anomalies. With Intune's compliance engine feeding device status into Azure AD, and tools like Microsoft Defender for Endpoint providing real-time threat intelligence, the stage is set for dynamic policy application. In this setup, each device or session can be assigned a risk level—low, medium, or high—based on factors like detected malware, suspicious sign-in patterns, or known vulnerabilities. If a device is deemed high risk, conditional access can automatically escalate login demands or block the session until the threat is resolved.

This methodology is particularly useful for high-value targets, such as administrators or those with elevated privileges. Security teams often impose baseline risk-level checks on privileged accounts, requiring them to pass stricter compliance gates or use hardware-based authentication methods. Regular user accounts might simply be prompted for MFA if their sign-in risk is medium, whereas high-risk logins are outright denied. Such gradations ensure that employees who routinely face advanced threats—like C-level leaders or IT administrators—are safeguarded by more potent rules, reducing the potential blast radius of a compromised account. By letting the risk engine dictate conditions in real time, you move away from static, one-size-fits-all policies toward a fluid defense posture that adapts to daily realities.

Examples of Custom Policies

To illustrate these ideas, imagine three sample policies administrators might create:

1. **Executive High-Security Policy**: A policy designed for C-suite and key decision-makers. It mandates disk encryption, demands the latest version of Windows or macOS, and enforces multi-factor authentication for every login attempt, regardless of the location. Additionally, if the device's risk level goes above "medium"—say, because Defender for Endpoint spotted a potential intrusion—it immediately triggers a conditional access block until the device is cleared. This ensures that the people who handle the most sensitive data encounter the strongest security measures.

2. **Traveling Sales Policy**: For sales representatives who frequently log in from airports, hotels, or overseas locations, this policy might permit access from untrusted IP ranges but requires additional proof of identity, such as an MFA prompt that uses a secure authenticator app. The devices must still meet standard compliance rules—like updated OS and active antivirus protection—but the policy stops short of requiring advanced encryption for every device because many sales reps use personally owned devices. While the risk is not as high as for executives, the policy remains robust enough to catch unauthorized or suspicious login attempts.

3. **Contractor Limited Access Policy**: Contractors or temporary workers might receive restricted access to only specific resources, such as a designated SharePoint site or project management tool. This policy can enforce a basic compliance requirement (like a valid antivirus and a minimum OS version) and block everything else by default. Because contractors might be connecting from personal devices or various client sites, location-based rules may be relaxed. However, to guard against data exfiltration, the policy might incorporate device risk checks and automatically log or restrict file download actions. This approach serves to protect the organization while ensuring contractors can still fulfill their responsibilities.

Managing Overlaps and Conflicts

When implementing multiple policies, overlaps or conflicts can arise. For instance, an executive might simultaneously belong to a "Finance" group and an "Executive" group, each with its own set of compliance policies. Intune and Azure AD generally apply the most restrictive settings from overlapping policies, but administrators should be aware that this might lead to unintended consequences. A device could be marked compliant by one policy but fail compliance checks in another, confusing end users who don't understand why they can access one set of resources but not another.

To manage such scenarios, it is wise to review policy assignments regularly, ensuring that groups are clearly defined and that each policy's rationale is documented. If the "why" behind a policy is unclear or outdated, administrators may find themselves saddled with extraneous rules that create friction with minimal security benefit. Periodic audits— perhaps quarterly or biannually—provide an opportunity to remove or update stale policies, align them with new compliance requirements, and adapt them to evolving threats or changes in organizational structure.

Communicating Customized Policies

A well-tailored set of policies only becomes effective if employees understand how they apply. This communication component is crucial, especially when certain groups face more stringent checks than others. The last thing an IT department wants is for executives to interpret repeated MFA prompts as a technical glitch, rather than a deliberate security measure. Similarly, contractors who try to access a restricted resource might incorrectly believe that their credentials are broken if they're not informed about their limited permissions.

For that reason, organizations that segment policies often pair them with targeted training or onboarding sessions. Executives might receive a short briefing about why strong encryption is mandatory for their devices. Remote workers get an FAQ that clarifies location-based checks and how to authenticate securely when traveling. This straightforward, role-specific communication cuts down on help desk calls and fosters goodwill, transforming security from an opaque burden into a transparent partnership.

The Strategic Edge

Ultimately, customizing policies based on roles, locations, and risk levels empowers organizations to adopt a targeted defense strategy rather than relying on uniform, top-heavy rules. This nuanced approach underscores the flexibility and power that Intune, Azure AD, and Microsoft's other security services bring to modern endpoint management. By aligning security measures with the realities of each group's workflow, you maintain higher levels of compliance, reduce friction, and achieve a better balance between safeguarding data and enabling productivity. Tailored policies also make it simpler to demonstrate regulatory alignment, as auditors can see that an organization not only sets security standards but applies them rationally to different user segments.

In a world where devices, data, and threats multiply daily, the ability to refine and target security measures stands out as a distinct advantage. Fine-tuning policies for specific roles or contexts helps ensure that sensitive tasks receive the protection they deserve, while more routine functions proceed without undue complication. This dynamic layering of security—one that evolves as roles shift or the workforce changes—offers both the responsiveness and resilience required for today's ever-changing business environments.

Chapter 6: Best Practices for Managing Policies in Intune

Policy Management and Organization

As an organization's number of devices and security requirements grow, so does the complexity of its Intune environment. Multiple compliance policies, configuration profiles, and conditional access rules can accumulate, each serving a specific purpose. Without thoughtful organization, you may struggle to determine which policies apply to which groups or inadvertently create conflicts that frustrate users. Taking a structured, methodical approach to policy management helps avoid chaos and confusion. In particular, naming conventions and documentation are vital tools for administrators seeking to keep track of their expanding ecosystem.

The Challenge of Scale

It's one thing to have a handful of compliance policies when you first roll out Intune, each addressing basic operating system updates or password complexity. However, as your organization's needs evolve, new policies arise to match them. Perhaps you introduce device-specific encryption rules for Windows laptops, while a separate policy enforces passcode requirements on iOS devices. Over time, you might add more nuanced rules, such as custom compliance checks for specialized hardware used by developers. Before you know it, the admin center can bristle with a dense patchwork of configurations.

When administrators fail to keep these expansions organized, it can cause a ripple effect of confusion and inefficiency. Users might receive conflicting prompts or discover that certain apps behave differently from one policy to the next. Trouble tickets often spike as employees attempt to reconcile contradictory device requirements. Meanwhile, security teams can't easily see which rules are effectively enforced and which may have become outdated. Eventually, this tangle of policies becomes not just a technical inconvenience but a potential security risk, as out-of-date

71

rules or overlapping configurations can create holes an attacker might exploit. Proper policy management—particularly around naming and documentation—helps ensure that each rule set remains purposeful, up-to-date, and easy to understand.

The Importance of Naming Conventions

One of the simplest, yet most frequently overlooked, methods of staying organized is to use consistent, descriptive naming conventions. In many companies, you'll find policy names like "Policy 1" or "Windows Compliance," which reveal almost nothing about the policy's scope, target group, or date of creation. Over time, these nondescript names compound the confusion. A better approach is to embed meaningful details directly into the policy name.

An effective naming convention typically includes references to the platform, the policy's purpose, and possibly the relevant group or department. For instance, you might adopt a format like "Platform – PolicyCategory – Detail – Version." Under this scheme, a policy name could be "Windows10_Compliance_EncryptionReq_v1" or "iOS_AppProtection_Marketing_v2." Immediately, any administrator scanning the list of policies knows which devices are affected, the type of configuration involved, and which version of the policy is active. Some organizations also include a short date or timestamp in their naming convention, indicating when the policy was last modified, such as "Windows10_Compliance_EncryptionReq_v1_2023-06-15." This extra layer can be especially helpful when policies undergo frequent revisions.

Some admins worry these more elaborate names clutter the admin console, but the clarity far outweighs any visual inconvenience. Rather than rummaging through each policy's settings to see if it applies to a specific scenario, you can glean that information immediately from the name. In time, you'll likely refine your conventions based on organizational structure. A multinational firm might add region or country indicators, e.g., "EMEA," "APAC," or "NA," to differentiate policies required by location-based regulations. The point is consistency: if every policy follows a reliable formula, you eliminate guesswork and significantly reduce the risk of applying the wrong policy to the wrong group.

Utilizing Groups and Hierarchies

Clear naming conventions go hand in hand with well-defined groups in Azure Active Directory (Azure AD). Even the best policy naming scheme won't help if your group structure is haphazard. Ideally, you create Azure AD groups that reflect meaningful segments of your user base—such as departments, roles, or device ownership models. For example, you might have groups like "Finance_WindowsDevices," "Sales_iOS," or "Developers_Android." By mapping each policy to a specific group or set of groups, you ensure that the rules remain consistent for those users or devices.

In larger enterprises, you might also adopt nested or dynamic groups to manage the complexities of user movement. A dynamic group for "All Windows 10 Devices" can automatically capture newly enrolled laptops, while a nested group for "Executives – Windows 10" can inherit broader Windows settings but layer on additional protections for that high-risk subset. Aligning your policy architecture with these hierarchical structures keeps your environment neat and makes troubleshooting simpler. If a user complains about unexpected security prompts, you can quickly verify which group memberships apply and which specific policies might be in play.

Documentation as a Living Record

Naming alone, while essential, only solves part of the puzzle. Each policy also needs detailed documentation, ideally in a central repository accessible to your entire IT or security team. This documentation can be as simple as a structured template stored in SharePoint or a knowledge management system. Alternatively, larger organizations might adopt more sophisticated tools designed for configuration management databases (CMDBs). Whichever medium you choose, the goal remains the same: to have a single source of truth describing each policy's purpose, scope, and change history.

At a minimum, thorough policy documentation should answer key questions:

1. **What is the purpose of this policy?**
   For instance, is it meant to enforce disk encryption on corporate-owned laptops or manage passcode complexity on mobile devices?

2. **Who is affected by it?**
   Which Azure AD groups or device types does it target?

3. **What are the key settings or compliance requirements?**
   Are you enforcing BitLocker on Windows or requiring a certain OS version for iOS?

4. **When was it last updated?**
   Maintaining a change log helps administrators see how the policy has evolved. If user complaints spike after a particular update, you can cross-reference the changes in your documentation.

5. **What are the known dependencies or conflicts?**
   Some policies work best in tandem; others may conflict if applied simultaneously. Documenting these relationships saves time when diagnosing issues.

The power of this living record comes to fruition when you make changes or hand over responsibilities. If your lead Intune administrator leaves, the next person can review the documentation and understand the rationale behind each policy. This continuity prevents the risk of losing institutional knowledge and fosters a culture where updates happen efficiently. Additionally, well-documented policies are often a requirement in regulated environments. During audits, you can demonstrate not just the technical enforcement via Intune, but also show how each policy is mapped to a documented need or compliance guideline.

Version Control and Policy Lifecycle

As your organization grows or external regulations change, policies will require revisions. Adopting version control ensures that you keep track of each update. Some administrators do this by appending version numbers to the policy name (as mentioned before), while others rely on in-document revision tracking. The key is consistency.

Let's say you modify a Windows compliance policy to require a newer version of Windows 10 because a recent vulnerability demands it. Mark the new iteration as "v2," note it in the documentation, and highlight the changes in the policy details. This process helps you roll back quickly if the update causes unforeseen compatibility issues or sparks user confusion. Rather than flailing around to figure out which settings changed, you have a record indicating precisely what was altered and why.

Additionally, policies can have lifespans. A security requirement for Windows 8 devices becomes irrelevant once everyone upgrades to Windows 10. Keeping stale policies around can lead to clutter and confusion. Periodic reviews—every six or twelve months—provide an opportunity to retire or consolidate outdated policies. During these reviews, the documentation itself can guide you to decisions about whether a policy has served its purpose or if it needs integration into a broader, more comprehensive rule set.

Streamlining Audits and Compliance Checks

Organized policy management extends beyond internal IT efficiency; it also bolsters external compliance. Many regulations require verifiable documentation explaining how you secure data or ensure devices meet specific standards. If an auditor requests proof that all corporate devices have disk encryption, you can quickly produce the relevant Intune policy documentation and the naming convention that clearly identifies its scope (e.g., "Windows10_Compliance_EncryptionReq_v3"). You might also reference reports showing which devices comply and how the policy is assigned. This methodic approach streamlines the entire audit process, reducing last-minute scrambles for evidence.

Moreover, if different regulations or client contracts require unique security postures, you can establish separate but complementary policies. An internal policy might address general corporate guidelines, while another is explicitly crafted to meet, say, HIPAA or PCI-DSS requirements. With a naming convention that flags these policies—"Windows10_PCI_Compliance_v2"—you quickly see which group of devices or users fulfill that special compliance. By layering these custom policies, you maintain clarity, ensuring each piece of regulatory or client-driven security is covered without conflating it with broader corporate rules.

Fostering a Policy-Focused Culture

Beyond the technical benefits, a well-structured policy environment fosters a culture that values clarity, accountability, and continuous improvement. Teams within the IT department learn the importance of naming, documenting, and regularly reviewing policies. When new hires join or existing staff transition roles, they can swiftly get up to speed by reading existing documentation, referencing policy names, and understanding the scope of each configuration. Users also benefit from consistent, predictable experiences across devices. Instead of receiving cryptic "Policy 1 applied" messages, they see references to a well-labeled policy that is easily explained by the help desk if needed.

Encouraging a policy-focused culture also means reinforcing guidelines for any new policy. For instance, if a developer or security analyst wants to introduce a new compliance requirement, they must adhere to the established naming structure and update the central documentation. This set of expectations prevents the old problem of "ad hoc policy" creation, where newcomers spin up arbitrary policies that clutter the environment. Over time, the practice of keeping thorough, organized records becomes second nature, leading to a more stable and secure environment.

Building a Strong Foundation

Effective policy management in Intune is about more than labeling and filing. It is the foundation upon which you build a secure, adaptive endpoint management strategy. Without coherent naming conventions, you risk drowning in ambiguous policy lists. Without structured documentation, you face confusion when updates inevitably occur, or when colleagues need to audit or refine a configuration. By investing time in naming, grouping, and documenting every policy, you lay the groundwork for an Intune ecosystem that can expand smoothly and handle new challenges without slipping into disorder.

This disciplined approach also yields dividends in user satisfaction and compliance. Employees generally prefer systems that operate seamlessly, free from conflicting rules or mysterious prompts. Regulators and auditors appreciate the transparency of seeing exactly how policies are set up, enforced, and retired. As you continue to refine your naming conventions and documentation practices, you transform Intune from a functional tool into a strategic asset, capable of adapting to your organization's evolving security landscape and supporting its growth for years to come.

Monitoring and Troubleshooting

Even the most carefully planned policies and configurations can hit roadblocks when they're deployed in live environments. Devices may fail to check in, users might experience unexpected prompts, and policy conflicts can emerge in ways that aren't immediately obvious. Microsoft Intune provides a suite of monitoring tools and dashboards to help administrators keep an eye on compliance, enrollment, and overall system health. By learning how to interpret these dashboards—and by adopting a structured approach to troubleshooting—you can resolve issues more quickly, reduce user frustration, and maintain a stable security posture.

The Evolving Nature of Troubleshooting

Troubleshooting in Intune is not a one-time event but an ongoing process. Policies evolve, operating systems receive frequent updates, and new devices constantly enter the environment. Each of these changes presents opportunities for minor misconfigurations or incompatibilities to arise. Hence, having a robust monitoring strategy is as important as planning your initial rollout. Monitoring tools, whether built into Intune or integrated from external solutions, serve as your early warning system, detecting deviations before they cascade into major problems. They also provide a retrospective lens, letting you see trends over time, such as recurring compliance failures on particular device models or spikes in access blocks due to policy changes.

Intune's Monitoring Tools and Dashboards

Most Intune administrators do their day-to-day monitoring in the Microsoft Endpoint Manager admin center, which offers a rich set of dashboards and reports. While these dashboards may appear overwhelming initially, each is designed to answer specific questions about your environment. Among the most commonly used dashboards are:

- **Device Compliance**: Offers a quick snapshot of how many devices are compliant versus non-compliant. By drilling deeper, you can see which policies are causing the most compliance failures and which devices consistently fail to meet requirements.

- **Enrollment Status**: Reflects how many devices have successfully enrolled in Intune, how many are pending, and which ones might have encountered enrollment errors. Enrollment issues often stem from incorrect credentials, device OS incompatibilities, or conflicting group memberships.

- **Configuration Profiles and Policy Assignments**: Shows whether profiles have applied successfully, are in progress, or have errored out. If a profile fails, the dashboard usually displays an error message or code that provides clues about the underlying problem.

- **App Management**: For administrators who deploy mobile apps or Windows applications through Intune, this dashboard indicates whether apps installed correctly, are pending installation, or failed to install. This helps you spot issues with application packaging or device OS versions that aren't compatible with certain apps.

- **Security Baselines**: For organizations that leverage Microsoft's predefined security baselines, this area indicates where each device stands relative to the recommended settings. Inconsistencies between a baseline and custom policies can often reveal misalignments you need to address.

Navigating these dashboards effectively means understanding not only the status indicators but also how each piece fits into your organization's larger policy framework. For example, if you see a surge in non-compliance for Windows devices right after rolling out a new disk encryption requirement, the timing suggests that the new requirement is causing the issue. Users might need more time or clearer instructions to enable BitLocker, or perhaps the policy conflicts with older hardware lacking a Trusted Platform Module (TPM).

Common Troubleshooting Scenarios

Many of the day-to-day issues you'll encounter in Intune fall into a handful of broad categories. Recognizing these scenarios helps you adopt a more methodical approach to troubleshooting and often leads to a faster resolution.

1. **Enrollment Failures**
   A device might refuse to enroll due to incorrect user credentials or a mismatch between the device's OS version and the policy's minimum requirements. Occasionally, stale Azure AD records can cause confusion, especially if a device was previously enrolled under a different user account. In such cases, deleting old device entries and having the user re-attempt enrollment can solve the problem. If errors persist, reviewing logs from the Company Portal app (on mobile) or the Intune Management Extension (on Windows) can pinpoint the error code or reason for failure.

2. **Compliance Discrepancies**
   Devices might show as non-compliant for reasons like missing OS updates, lacking encryption, or failing a specific configuration requirement. Often, the user is simply unaware of the setting they need to fix, so sending a friendly reminder helps. In more complicated scenarios, the policy might contradict another group policy from an on-premises environment (if you still use co-

management). Checking which policy actually "wins" the settings conflict is essential. Sometimes, reconfiguring group policy objects (GPOs) to avoid overlap with Intune is the best path forward.

3. **Conditional Access Blocks**

   Users may complain they cannot access email or corporate apps, triggering immediate concern. If you have set up conditional access policies tied to device compliance, non-compliance automatically leads to blocked access. The first step is confirming that the device is recognized as compliant in Intune; if not, the user must remediate the compliance issue. If the device is indeed compliant, investigate whether conditional access is seeing out-of-date signals—sometimes a delay or synchronization issue can cause Azure AD to believe the device is still non-compliant. Reviewing Azure AD sign-in logs can clarify whether the device's sign-in attempt was flagged as risky, or if other factors like a newly blocked location triggered the block.

4. **App Deployment Problems**

   When users report that an app never installed or keeps failing, consult the App Management dashboard. Sometimes, the device might not meet the system requirements for the app, or the user's device is associated with a different Azure AD group than the one targeted for the app deployment. If an error code appears, Intune documentation often provides a direct explanation or recommended solution steps. In some cases, testing the app installation manually on a pilot device can help confirm whether the app package itself is correctly configured.

5. **Profile or Setting Conflicts**

   A device might exhibit strange behavior because it receives overlapping profiles that set contradictory settings. For example, one profile might disable camera usage while another explicitly enables it. Intune generally applies the most restrictive setting, but the resulting user experience can be confusing. Reviewing the assigned profiles on the device in the Endpoint Manager admin center can reveal any conflicts. To fix this, you may need to consolidate or refine how profiles are assigned, ensuring that only one definitive rule exists for each setting per user or device group.

A Structured Troubleshooting Approach

When faced with an issue, it helps to have a structured plan. Begin by identifying whether the problem is user-specific, device-specific, or policy-wide. A single device that fails enrollment might point to user credentials or device settings, whereas a wave of compliance failures across multiple users suggests a broader policy or configuration error. Next, consult the relevant Intune dashboard to see any errors or warnings; these are your clues to the root cause.

Additionally, consider the timeline. If the issue surfaced right after you implemented a new setting or updated a policy, it's logical to start investigating there. Intune's audit logs can be especially insightful, as they record who changed what and when. For deeper diagnostic information, you can also gather device logs through the Company Portal or via the Microsoft Endpoint Manager admin center. While analyzing logs may seem technical and time-consuming, it frequently pinpoints the exact step where a failure occurs, leading to a targeted fix.

If you suspect a synchronization problem between Intune and Azure AD, or between Intune and Microsoft Defender for Endpoint, check the health status of these services in the Microsoft 365 admin center. Sometimes, transient network or service outages can cause synchronization lags that resolve themselves after a few hours. In more persistent cases, re-authenticating the service connectors might be necessary, or you may need to contact Microsoft support for back-end issues.

Leveraging Advanced Tools and Integrations

Beyond Intune's native dashboards, larger enterprises often rely on expanded monitoring tools. Microsoft Sentinel, for example, can ingest logs from Intune, Azure AD, Microsoft Defender for Endpoint, and other solutions. Sentinel's correlation capabilities may help you discover that many compliance failures align with specific Windows updates or geographic regions. Similarly, using Azure Monitor or Power BI to visualize Intune data can provide at-a-glance graphs and alerts that signal emerging issues.

For example, an administrator might configure a Power BI dashboard that tracks monthly compliance trends by department. If marketing's compliance rate dips below a certain threshold, an automated alert triggers, prompting further investigation. This approach transforms troubleshooting from a reactive exercise into a proactive process, where you discover potential trouble before it proliferates. Meanwhile, the security team might cross-reference Sentinel logs showing attempted cyberattacks with Intune data on device patch levels. If a wave of exploit attempts coincides with older OS builds, you have a clear call to accelerate OS updates for at-risk devices.

Communicating with End Users

A frequently overlooked facet of troubleshooting is end-user communication. Users often interpret "non-compliant" messages or blocked access notifications as system errors, rather than legitimate security controls. Educating employees on basic troubleshooting steps—such as verifying OS updates, checking their device enrollment status, or ensuring Wi-Fi connectivity—can dramatically reduce the help desk load. Simple online resources like FAQs, knowledge-base articles, or short video tutorials can empower users to resolve routine issues themselves.

When more complicated problems surface, a quick conversation might reveal that the user installed a third-party security tool conflicting with Intune's management or that they inadvertently disabled encryption while reorganizing their device's storage. By hearing the user's perspective, you can often piece together the puzzle faster than by analyzing logs alone. Although technical data is invaluable, human context can point you in the right direction, especially if you suspect a unique or isolated user action caused the problem.

The Value of Continuous Improvement

Monitoring and troubleshooting in Intune should be viewed as iterative processes tied closely to policy evolution. Each time you solve an issue, take a moment to ask: could we update our policies or user training to prevent this from recurring? Perhaps the problem stems from an overlooked scenario, like employees traveling internationally who can't always install OS updates on public Wi-Fi. Adjusting the policy to include a small grace period or providing an offline update mechanism could preempt future calls to the help desk. Over time, these small refinements accumulate into a more resilient system.

Additionally, keep an eye on the bigger picture. Regularly review whether your dashboards still capture all the relevant metrics or if new threats or organizational shifts require additional monitoring. A policy that worked flawlessly last year might cause friction after a major OS release or a wave of new hires with differing device preferences. In short, adopting a "monitor, learn, adjust" cycle ensures Intune remains aligned with both security needs and user requirements.

A Pillar of Effective Management

Monitoring and troubleshooting serve as the backbone of any mature Intune deployment. While the platform offers robust compliance and access control features, issues will inevitably arise as new devices, users, and policies come online. By leveraging Intune's built-in dashboards— and, if needed, integrating external solutions like Microsoft Sentinel or Power BI—administrators gain the visibility and diagnostic tools needed to keep the environment in equilibrium.

A structured troubleshooting method that starts with identifying the scope of the problem, uses dashboard insights, and taps into device logs or user feedback usually leads to swift resolutions. Pairing this technical approach with clear communication and continuous policy refinement transforms troubleshooting from a disruptive fire drill into a routine part of effective device management. In the end, a well-monitored Intune environment stands as a testament to diligent oversight, proactive problem-solving, and a commitment to maintaining the security and productivity that modern organizations demand.

Avoiding Common Pitfalls

Even with ample planning, thorough documentation, and a structured approach to policy management, it's remarkably easy to stumble into mistakes that can compromise the stability and effectiveness of your Intune environment. Some of these pitfalls arise from overlooking how different policies intersect, while others stem from inadequate communication or rushed rollouts. By understanding the most frequent missteps, administrators can steer clear of unnecessary headaches and maintain a well-functioning system that supports organizational goals without compromising security. Equally important is learning how to keep policies fresh as devices, operating systems, and user needs evolve—a process that calls for ongoing vigilance and a willingness to adapt.

1. Overlapping or Conflicting Policies

One of the most common pitfalls emerges when administrators create multiple policies that inadvertently overlap. Consider a scenario in which one policy requires a certain minimum OS version for Windows devices, while another demands an even stricter version threshold for the same group of users. Intune generally applies the more restrictive setting, but the result can confuse end users, especially if they see conflicting compliance messages or sudden blocks on resources. Similarly, having two configuration profiles that specify contradictory VPN settings can leave a device in limbo, repeatedly toggling between configurations.

The best remedy is to map each policy's scope carefully before deploying it. Assigning policies to distinct Azure Active Directory (Azure AD) groups, each representing unique business or security needs, helps avoid double coverage. Regularly auditing your policy environment can also highlight redundancies. Some companies schedule a quarterly policy review, where administrators compare each policy and group assignment to see if overlaps make sense or if they are the byproduct of ad-hoc updates over time. Whenever a new policy is created, it should be tested in a pilot group first—this step often reveals conflicts with existing settings that you can resolve prior to a full rollout.

2. Ignoring User Experience

Another frequent misstep is underestimating the impact of new or changed policies on user workflows. While security is a paramount concern, overly aggressive or poorly communicated rules can spark user frustration and lead to workarounds that defeat your security goals. A striking example is when an organization abruptly mandates disk encryption and demands it be enabled within a tight timeframe without warning employees. Users might suddenly find themselves unable to access critical files or facing lengthy encryption processes at inconvenient times, resulting in resentment and a flood of support tickets.

Ideally, any significant policy shift should come with a communication plan. Provide advance notice via email or internal announcements that explains why the change is happening, its timeline, and any steps users need to take. Some administrators go further, creating a quick "how-to" guide for enabling certain settings—like BitLocker on Windows or FileVault on macOS—so that the transition feels less intimidating. Engaging key departments or user groups in a pilot can also provide early feedback, helping you refine the policy to better suit real-world needs before it goes live across the organization.

3. Over-Reliance on Default Settings

Microsoft Intune and related services like Azure AD offer out-of-the-box configurations designed to meet common needs. While these can serve as helpful starting points, treating them as a perfect fit for your unique environment is risky. Each organization has distinct risk tolerances, compliance obligations, and user workflows. Relying solely on default settings might result in security gaps or missed opportunities to streamline the user experience. For instance, Intune provides a basic compliance policy requiring a device password, but your particular compliance mandate might require multi-factor authentication for certain roles or a more rigorous encryption level.

To avoid this pitfall, organizations should treat default policies as templates rather than final solutions. Study each default setting in detail: is it too lenient or too restrictive for your context? Does it align with specific industry regulations—like HIPAA or PCI-DSS—that your company must satisfy? By customizing these baseline settings with your enterprise's requirements in mind, you create policies that are both tailored and stable. Whenever Microsoft releases updated best practices or new security baselines, evaluate them critically rather than adopting them blindly. Over time, this hands-on approach fosters a deeper understanding of Intune's capabilities, enabling more nuanced policy creation.

4. Neglecting Documentation and Version Control

A lack of systematic documentation is perhaps the most pervasive mistake. Policies evolve, admins come and go, and without a clear record of why a given policy was introduced or how it changed over time, it becomes difficult to troubleshoot or justify certain security decisions. For example, administrators might remove a setting they deem redundant, only to discover later it was crucial for another department's workflow or for meeting a particular regulatory requirement. Without version control, reverting to an earlier state can be time-consuming or impossible.

To address this, create a standardized template for documenting each policy. Note its purpose, the target group, key settings, and references to any compliance mandates. If you adjust a policy, increment the version number and explain the reason for the change in a short log entry. This practice ensures that new administrators understand the history of each configuration, and it can be invaluable during audits. Although it may require extra effort initially, this discipline pays dividends by maintaining clarity and accountability.

5. Inadequate Testing and Pilots

Some organizations roll out major Intune policy changes to the entire company at once, reasoning that it saves time. In reality, this approach can lead to widespread disruptions if an overlooked conflict or misconfiguration goes live. The safer and ultimately more efficient path is to test changes with a small but representative group of users—a pilot program. This segment might include different device types, roles, and geographic regions to capture a variety of use cases. By observing how well the policy performs, you can gather feedback, identify potential issues, and refine configurations before broad deployment.

If the pilot experiences minimal turbulence, you can proceed to expand the policy's reach. Conversely, if participants report frequent compliance failures or unexpected user friction, you have valuable data to guide adjustments. Piloting is especially crucial when introducing new conditional access rules, as an error could inadvertently lock out essential services for many employees. A bit of upfront caution often averts operational chaos.

Maintaining Policy Compliance Over Time

Once you have a stable policy environment, the challenge shifts to keeping compliance high in a landscape that never stops changing. Operating systems release updates that can introduce new security settings or deprecate old ones. Devices age, new device models appear, and your workforce might expand or pivot in focus. Over time, these changes can render an originally well-crafted policy incomplete or irrelevant.

To stay current, many administrators adopt a cyclical process of periodic review and adjustment. In addition to the quarterly or biannual policy audits, they pay attention to upcoming OS releases and major application updates. If Windows announces a new feature that can improve device security, you might draft a policy to enforce that feature once it's tested. The same logic applies if Microsoft introduces updated security baselines for Intune—examine them and decide if adopting their recommendations (or only parts of them) is wise for your environment.

Regularly consulting user feedback is equally important. If employees frequently run into compliance blocks due to a particular rule, it may suggest that the rule needs refining or that users require better training. For instance, a policy requiring devices to be updated within two weeks of a major OS release might be sensible for most employees, but could prove overly aggressive for a specialized development team using software that takes longer to become compatible with new OS versions. By listening to user experiences, you can fine-tune the policy to strike a balance between security and practicality.

The Role of Automation

Organizations with larger Intune deployments often take advantage of automation to sustain policy compliance at scale. For instance, you might use Azure Logic Apps or Power Automate to send proactive alerts whenever a subset of devices falls below a certain compliance threshold. Some admins schedule automated scripts to check for newly enrolled devices that lack certain apps or configurations, then prompt users to remedy the shortfall.

You can also automate auditing tasks by exporting Intune compliance data to services like Microsoft Sentinel or Power BI. Visualization tools can highlight trends—like persistent non-compliance among a certain department or repeated blocks triggered by a single conditional access rule. By combining automated detection with a human review, you ensure that potential issues are flagged early and evaluated by someone who can decide whether a policy tweak or more training is the correct fix.

Balancing Stringency and Flexibility

A persistent theme in policy management is the tension between robust security and user convenience. Too lenient, and you invite vulnerabilities; too strict, and you create friction that often leads to shadow IT or user pushback. Successful Intune deployments strike a balance by gradually raising security bars in a transparent and supportive manner. Users accept stricter requirements if they understand the rationale, receive clear instructions, and see that administration remains open to feedback.

When administrators succumb to the temptation of one-size-fits-all policies, they risk damaging productivity in departments with unique operational demands. Conversely, rolling out an array of highly specialized policies for each micro-scenario can create an unmanageable sprawl. The ideal is somewhere in between: broad categories of policies that cover most scenarios, augmented by a few special configurations for users or devices requiring additional protection.

Nurturing a Resilient Environment

Avoiding common pitfalls in Intune configuration and ensuring long-term policy compliance are all about foresight, organization, and continuous improvement. Administrators who take the time to define thoughtful naming conventions, pilot test new rules, document changes, and regularly reevaluate policies will find their Intune environment running smoothly. Conversely, those who hastily deploy default configurations, neglect user feedback, or let dozens of overlapping policies accumulate risk creating more problems than they solve.

In a rapidly shifting digital ecosystem, today's best practice can quickly become tomorrow's liability. Nonetheless, by keeping a keen eye on emerging technologies, engaging in regular policy audits, and remembering to factor user experience into every decision, you can transform policy management into a strategic advantage. Ultimately, a well-maintained Intune environment strengthens your organization's security posture while empowering employees to work productively—an equilibrium that most IT teams strive for but few consistently achieve. By learning from these common mistakes and adopting a forward-thinking, adaptive approach, you ensure that your policies remain aligned with both current threats and future opportunities.

Chapter 7: The Future of Compliance and Conditional Access with Intune

Emerging Trends and Features

Over the past few years, Microsoft Intune and Azure Active Directory (Azure AD) have matured into essential tools for organizations seeking robust compliance and access control. Yet, as the cybersecurity landscape evolves and new technologies appear, these platforms continue to evolve as well. Microsoft's investment in artificial intelligence (AI) and machine learning (ML) has begun to reshape how Intune administrators manage devices, detect threats, and craft policies that adapt in near real time. At the same time, upcoming features promise to streamline some of the more labor-intensive aspects of endpoint management, providing additional layers of insight and automation. Understanding where these services are headed can help you future-proof your strategy and ensure that your policies align with tomorrow's challenges—not just today's.

The Drive Toward Greater Automation

One of the most prominent trends involves automating tasks that have traditionally been manual and time-consuming. Already, Intune provides automated enrollment, compliance checks, and even some remediation steps. Yet, future iterations of the service hint at deeper automation, particularly around device updates, risk-based restrictions, and application deployments. For instance, Microsoft has been testing more advanced patch automation features that let administrators define not just a deployment window but also fallback plans if a patch fails, reducing the risk of broad disruptions. Coupled with Azure AD's conditional access, these automated workflows can swiftly isolate any device that misses critical updates, preventing it from accessing corporate data until it's back in compliance.

Additionally, there is a push toward enabling "zero-touch" provisioning across a broader range of device types. The concept is simple: a new device arrives at an employee's desk, and after connecting to the network, it automatically configures itself through Intune, pulling down the right apps, security policies, and personalization settings based on the user's role. This approach aims to free IT teams from repetitive setup tasks, cutting deployment time drastically while also ensuring that devices conform to corporate standards from the moment they power on. Although zero-touch provisioning is already possible for certain hardware and vendors, upcoming enhancements in Intune may offer a more consistent, cross-platform experience.

Next-Generation Conditional Access

Conditional access has always been about making intelligent decisions at the point of sign-in or resource access, but future developments in Azure AD focus on refining that intelligence. Today, many organizations rely on standard signals like user credentials, device compliance, and geographic location to shape conditional access rules. However, Microsoft has indicated that more dynamic attributes will soon play a larger role. These attributes could include real-time threat intelligence sourced from multiple endpoints, historical context about a user's activity patterns, or the reputation of a particular connection method.

Imagine a scenario in which Azure AD identifies that a user's account is behaving differently than usual—perhaps by logging in at a time when they never have before, or repeatedly requesting access to systems that fall outside their typical workflows. Rather than solely relying on a static "blocked" or "allowed" decision, the next generation of conditional access might prompt for additional identity verification or temporarily limit the user's permissions. Such granular, adaptive responses have long been talked about in zero-trust strategies. Advancements in Azure AD's rule-engine—often driven by AI and ML—will make these dynamic policies increasingly practical, nudging security ever closer to a continuous verification model.

AI-Driven Threat Detection and Remediation

Microsoft has been investing heavily in AI to help detect threats across endpoints, networks, and cloud services. This is most visible in tools like

Microsoft Defender for Endpoint, which already leverages machine learning to identify unusual device behaviors and suspicious file executions. As the integration between Defender for Endpoint and Intune grows tighter, the AI-driven insights gleaned from endpoints will likely flow more seamlessly into Intune's compliance engine. When AI detects a high-probability threat on a specific laptop—perhaps a zero-day exploit that bypasses conventional antivirus measures—it can mark that device as high-risk. Intune can respond by labeling the device non-compliant and thus triggering a conditional access block.

Looking ahead, Microsoft's roadmap suggests even deeper reliance on machine learning models that examine not just individual devices but entire behavioral patterns across an organization's user base. These models could learn what "normal" means for each department, or even for specific roles. If someone in the finance department suddenly downloads developer-focused software or attempts to access code repositories they've never touched before, the system might consider that a suspicious anomaly, automatically limiting their permissions or notifying the security team. This level of contextual analysis amplifies traditional security controls, making them more precise and timely.

Policy Recommendations and Self-Optimizing Security

Another area where AI is set to influence Intune and Azure AD is in policy recommendations. Already, certain Microsoft 365 and Azure services offer "Secure Score" features, suggesting configurations that could strengthen your security stance based on industry best practices. Future versions of Intune may extend a similar concept to device and compliance policies, analyzing your existing settings and comparing them to both Microsoft's baselines and data gleaned from the broader ecosystem. If your Windows devices are, for example, frequently missing critical patches or encryption is only partially enforced, Intune could suggest policy adjustments, highlight the potential security gains, and estimate the user impact before you commit.

Over time, this could evolve into a form of self-optimizing security, where AI proactively adjusts rules or fine-tunes conditional access conditions to maintain a predefined risk threshold. While such capabilities would require cautious oversight—no one wants a rogue AI locking down the environment unexpectedly—they hold promise for organizations that want to maintain an agile security posture without constantly micromanaging each setting.

Expanded Platform Support and Integration

As organizations diversify their device fleets, Microsoft has shown growing interest in supporting a wide array of operating systems and hardware types. Linux, while historically peripheral in many corporate settings, has gained traction in developer environments and certain high-security contexts. Though Intune's Linux support is still evolving, rumors and early announcements suggest more robust management features could be on the horizon. If these enhancements materialize, administrators could apply compliance checks—like kernel version or mandatory disk encryption—to Linux devices and weave that data into the broader Intune compliance tapestry. This would fill a gap for companies that rely on open-source operating systems for specific tasks.

Integration doesn't stop at operating systems, either. Many organizations utilize multiple security tools—firewalls, SIEM solutions, vulnerability scanners—from various vendors. Microsoft has been pushing for an open ecosystem where Intune and Azure AD exchange signals with external services. A prime example is how certain third-party mobile threat defense solutions already share device risk statuses with Intune. As AI matures, the ability to pull in more diverse data sets—like advanced phishing detection from a specialized vendor—could lead to richer decision-making in conditional access and compliance policies.

The Rise of Identity Governance

Closely related to device and application management is the realm of identity governance, which ensures that users have the right access at the right times—and no more. Azure AD already offers features like entitlement management, access reviews, and privileged identity management. However, the future likely holds tighter alignment between identity governance and Intune's compliance policies. Picture a scenario where an access review automatically triggers device compliance checks before renewing a user's membership in a sensitive Azure AD group. If the user's device doesn't meet the newly required security standards, the group membership—and thus the user's ability to access certain resources—could be revoked until compliance is restored. This forms a cohesive lifecycle where identity rights, device state, and conditional access interlock to minimize risk and maintain regulatory alignment.

The Human Element in AI-Driven Systems

While AI and machine learning can drastically enhance the speed and accuracy of security decisions, they don't remove the need for human judgment. Administrators must remain vigilant about potential false positives—instances where AI flags harmless behaviors as suspicious. Suppose an executive occasionally works with a development team on a unique project. If AI sees that as anomalous behavior, it might block legitimate work. Balancing automation with human oversight becomes critical, especially if you adopt advanced self-optimizing or self-remediating policies.

Moreover, ethical considerations come into play when analyzing user behaviors. While advanced models can detect internal threats more effectively, they also might capture data about employees' daily tasks, raising privacy concerns. Organizations must weigh the benefits of heightened security against potential overreach or the appearance of excessive surveillance. Transparent communication and well-defined policies about what data is collected and how it's used will remain paramount, even as the technology grows more sophisticated.

Future-Ready Preparation

How can organizations prepare for these emerging features and AI-driven transformations? Part of the answer lies in cultivating a flexible, forward-looking mindset. Administrators who stay abreast of Microsoft's product roadmaps, attend relevant webinars or conferences, and test preview releases gain a first-mover advantage in adapting to new capabilities. Likewise, refining your baseline policies to be as clear and modular as possible can make it easier to layer on advanced AI features as they become available.

Investing in skills development also matters. While Intune's interface is designed to simplify policy management, advanced AI features may require a deeper grasp of conditional logic, data analysis, and integration with other cloud services. Security professionals who understand how to interpret machine learning results, manage false positives, and tune models will stand out in a workforce increasingly shaped by AI.

On the user side, preparing for these advancements often means reinforcing trust and transparency. If employees understand that AI is an additional layer that helps protect corporate and personal data—rather than a spying mechanism—they're more likely to cooperate. Providing training on how these new systems work, and giving users ways to quickly flag if something goes awry, fosters a culture of collaboration rather than compliance by coercion.

A Constantly Evolving Frontier

The future of Intune and Azure AD is set on a path of deeper intelligence, broader automation, and ever-closer integration with other security tools. AI and machine learning sit at the heart of this shift, promising a level of proactive defense and real-time adaptation that far surpasses manual policy enforcement. Organizations that embrace these innovations cautiously—balancing the need for human oversight and ethical considerations—will likely find themselves better equipped to handle emerging threats in a zero-trust world.

Simultaneously, expanded support for diverse platforms and enhanced features in conditional access underscore Microsoft's aim to serve as a one-stop solution for enterprise-grade endpoint management. Whether you run a multinational corporation with thousands of devices or a specialized lab with unique hardware, Intune's roadmap suggests an increasing ability to tailor and automate security to fit your exact needs. As AI refines the details, administrators can expect not just more data, but more actionable insights, freeing them to focus on strategic decisions rather than slogging through minutiae. Indeed, for those willing to learn and adapt, the future of Intune and Azure AD heralds a new era of agile, intelligent security—a wave that's already underway and poised to transform how organizations safeguard their digital frontiers.

Preparing for Continuous Change

Adapting to the rapid evolution of Microsoft's services requires not just technical expertise, but also a willingness to embrace lifelong learning. The pace of updates in Intune, Azure Active Directory (Azure AD), and related security technologies can feel dizzying: new features are added in monthly release cycles, best practices shift with the emergence of new threats, and entire paradigms—like zero trust—continue to refine themselves in real time. Organizations that rest on their laurels and treat device management as a static process risk losing ground to malicious actors who exploit gaps in outdated security controls. To remain effective, administrators, managers, and security professionals must cultivate habits of continuous education—seeking out updates, exploring pre-release tools, and connecting with a network of peers who can share insights and warn of pitfalls.

The Importance of Staying Current

Even a fundamental feature like device compliance can radically change over a few Intune updates. One month you might have basic OS version checks, and the next, Microsoft releases a new baseline that ups the ante on encryption or password complexity. These shifts can break existing workflows if you deploy them abruptly or fail to communicate the changes to end users. Conversely, ignoring such updates can mean missing out on advanced functionality that might simplify your environment, automate tasks, or address emerging security threats. In practical terms, this means you need reliable methods for keeping up with the service roadmap and verifying how new features work before pushing them into production.

More than just a matter of technical curiosity, staying current is part of good governance. Regulatory environments evolve, too. Governments and international bodies frequently introduce or revise data protection laws, turning yesterday's "optional" feature into today's mandatory compliance requirement. If you only revisit your Intune policies once every few years, you may find yourself scrambling to align with new rules under tight deadlines, risking hefty fines or reputational damage. Regularly reviewing available updates, features, and best practices protects both your organization's data and its regulatory standing.

Official Microsoft Resources

Microsoft invests considerable effort in documentation, training portals, and forums. At the center of this ecosystem are the Microsoft Learn resources, which include free modules and learning paths on everything from basic Intune administration to advanced zero-trust strategies. These guided lessons often include hands-on labs that let you practice in a sandbox environment—an excellent way to test new features or configurations without putting your production system at risk. As you progress, you can tackle more specialized courses or aim for certifications like Microsoft's Mobility and Security path, which validate your Intune expertise.

For those seeking a higher-level overview, the official Microsoft Docs site (docs.microsoft.com) provides a continuously updated repository of how-to guides, API references, and conceptual articles. This platform also houses details on upcoming releases or deprecations of certain features. Keeping an eye on these announcements can avert surprises when a beloved configuration setting changes or an entire legacy feature is removed in favor of a newer approach. If time permits, subscribing to documentation pages or using RSS feeds can help you quickly skim newly published items. Some administrators even schedule a weekly or monthly block of time to check for announcements, ensuring they remain informed about the evolving functionalities.

Insider and Preview Programs

Microsoft frequently offers preview or insider programs that grant early access to upcoming capabilities. For instance, the Intune Public Preview program allows administrators to test new features in a controlled environment. Engaging with these previews not only gives you a head start on mastering future tools, but it also provides Microsoft with valuable feedback. If you discover an issue or have suggestions for improvements, your input can shape the final release, often making the general availability version more stable for everyone.

Participating in these programs demands a level of caution: previews can introduce bugs or incomplete features that might disrupt production if you enable them prematurely. However, setting up a test tenant or a dedicated pilot group can mitigate these risks. By seeing how your environment interacts with pre-release features, you can develop strategies for rolling them out safely when they become stable. This proactive approach reflects a shift from merely reacting to changes to actively helping shape them.

Community Engagement

Beyond official channels, countless professionals worldwide share experiences, troubleshooting tips, and success stories through community forums, blogs, and social media. The Microsoft Tech Community is a prominent gathering place, hosting dedicated areas for Intune, Azure AD, and security practices. Here you can find detailed discussion threads on niche topics, from script-based device management to advanced application packaging. Community members often post step-by-step guides, code snippets, and real-world case studies that can clarify scenarios the official docs might only hint at.

User groups and community conferences—even virtual meetups—can also be a goldmine of knowledge. Microsoft hosts events like Microsoft Ignite, where product teams unveil new capabilities, lead interactive workshops, and address common user questions in real time. Many large cities have local user groups that convene regularly to discuss endpoint management, share success stories, and troubleshoot collectively. Joining these groups can expand your professional network, introducing you to people who have encountered and solved the very issues you're grappling with. The intangible value of these personal connections often shines through in crisis moments, when a quick direct message to a knowledgeable peer can save hours of frustration.

Staying Ahead of Threats with Security Intelligence

In a constantly changing threat landscape, relying solely on official announcements and user forums might not suffice. Security intelligence platforms—like Microsoft 365 Defender or Microsoft Sentinel—feed threat updates directly to your dashboards, alerting you when malicious campaigns or vulnerabilities start trending. By correlating these threat signals with your Intune compliance data, you get a dynamic view of how emerging risks might affect your endpoints. If a new ransomware strain specifically targets older OS versions, for example, you can tighten compliance rules or accelerate patch rollouts in response.

While these platforms offer automated detection and remediation, human expertise remains critical. Attending security-focused webinars or workshops can deepen your understanding of how advanced adversaries operate, equipping you with strategies to fortify your Intune environment. Combining real-time threat intelligence with an informed security mindset places you in a stronger position to adapt policies quickly, rather than reacting in panic when an attack is underway.

Building a Culture of Continuous Learning

It's not enough for a few IT personnel to remain informed; an organization's overall culture should support ongoing education about security and compliance. Leaders can champion a policy of continuous improvement, recognizing that part of every administrator's job is to track developments in Intune and related services. Allowing time and budget for training, certifications, and community involvement sends a clear message: the company values up-to-date expertise and sees it as foundational to mitigating risks.

At an operational level, scheduling regular knowledge-sharing sessions can ensure that insights gleaned from events, previews, or user groups spread across the team. Perhaps one administrator attends a virtual conference on advanced conditional access strategies, then organizes a lunch-and-learn session to relay highlights and demonstrate new techniques. This approach fosters collective advancement. Instead of confining knowledge to a single expert who might leave the company, you invest in a team that grows together, cross-pollinating best practices along the way.

Navigating Organizational Change

Apart from technological shifts, organizational upheaval—mergers, acquisitions, leadership turnovers—can also affect how you manage Intune. Sudden expansions in user count might push you to re-evaluate your group structures, while new executive directives may shift the balance between security strictness and user convenience. In these circumstances, being nimble is critical. If your policies and processes are documented, flexible, and informed by the latest Microsoft capabilities, you'll be better poised to adapt to new demands, whether they involve scaling up, consolidating multiple Intune tenants, or adopting a fresh compliance framework.

Additionally, robust communication channels with stakeholders help. C-suite leaders or department heads often decide on budget allocations or compliance targets. If you can articulate how recent enhancements in Intune—like AI-driven threat intelligence or advanced analytics—will satisfy business goals or regulatory needs, you're more likely to secure the resources you need. On the flip side, if you neglect to keep up with these advancements, you may struggle to convince stakeholders to invest in what they see as an aging or insufficient security platform.

Personalizing Your Learning Path

Everyone's path to staying current looks different. Some administrators find it most effective to read official release notes and test updates in a private lab environment. Others thrive on social interaction, regularly attending meetups and networking with subject-matter experts. Yet others prefer structured learning paths and official certifications, seeing them as milestones that prove mastery to both themselves and their employers. Experiment with these methods to discover what fits best with your schedule, your learning style, and the specific responsibilities you hold.

A balanced approach often works well. You might spend one afternoon a week browsing new posts on the Microsoft Tech Community, keep an eye on official release notes, and set aside an hour monthly to experiment with at least one new feature in a test environment. Periodically, you could attend a local or virtual conference, or enroll in an online course if a major Intune overhaul looms. By blending these resources and pacing yourself, you establish a rhythm that avoids burnout while ensuring you remain cognizant of critical updates.

Embracing an Evolving Future

Preparing for continuous change in Intune and Azure AD is not simply about following the latest release cycle or patch update. It's about adopting a mindset that expects and even welcomes ongoing evolution, understanding that technology will keep shifting as threats become more cunning, user demands grow more diverse, and regulatory frameworks grow more intricate. By tapping into Microsoft's official resources, engaging with community experts, and aligning your learning habits with the organization's broader security posture, you equip yourself to navigate these shifts with confidence.

Staying current isn't just about maintaining a skill set—it's about upholding a dynamic defense that protects your data, your users, and your strategic objectives. Each new feature, each community insight, and each successful pilot test of a preview release represents another step forward. Rather than viewing Intune and Azure AD as static tools, treat them as living platforms that can be shaped and optimized continually. Embracing this evolving nature allows you to not merely keep pace with change but to transform it into a competitive advantage, where security becomes a source of agility and innovation rather than a burdensome afterthought.

Reflecting on the Journey with Intune

Every meaningful expedition has key milestones—moments that force us to pause, take stock, and decide how to move forward. As you conclude this book on compliance and access control with Microsoft Intune, it's worth looking back at the major steps you've taken. From defining the bedrock of compliance policies to orchestrating advanced conditional access strategies, you've explored how Intune and its ecosystem of security services can safeguard your organization's data. Just as important, you've gained insights into structuring policies, engaging stakeholders, and leveraging AI-driven capabilities that shape modern security.

Revisiting the Core Themes

At the outset, you learned how essential compliance policies are to any security posture. They operate as your first line of defense, ensuring that devices follow minimum standards: up-to-date operating systems, enforced encryption, strong passcodes, and so on. Recognizing that organizations now extend across physical offices, home environments, and remote corners of the world, compliance policies unify these diverse endpoints under a single framework. They set the ground rules, defining what it means to be "safe" and how devices should function in a corporate environment.

These policies lead naturally to conditional access, which transforms compliance from a static checklist into a real-time gatekeeper. Rather than trusting a device simply because it's on your network, conditional access ensures that a device remains trustworthy on an ongoing basis. Integrating Intune with Azure Active Directory means that each login attempt can be evaluated for risk factors. If a device is non-compliant or exhibits high-risk behavior, access is denied until the problem is resolved. The underlying logic rests on zero trust: no user or device is beyond scrutiny, and every access attempt requires validation against current, contextual intelligence.

The middle chapters delved deeper into creating, assigning, and monitoring policies—steps that can become unruly without proper planning. You learned that naming conventions, documentation, and structured pilot rollouts aren't just "nice to have," but indispensable for keeping complex configurations in line. The stories showcased companies grappling with everything from overlapping policies to user adoption hurdles, and showed how carefully targeted communication or a small pilot group can preempt more significant issues. Continual monitoring, coupled with the ability to troubleshoot effectively, rounds out the day-to-day management cycle, ensuring that compliance remains stable as devices come and go.

Building on these fundamentals, you discovered how Intune integrates with other Microsoft security tools to form a cohesive, automated, and intelligent environment. Solutions like Microsoft Defender for Endpoint feed real-time threat intelligence back into Intune's compliance engine, automatically flagging compromised devices. Meanwhile, Azure AD conditional access, bolstered by AI, fosters risk-based access decisions that adapt to user context and behavior. The synergy of these services lets you manage a sprawling, heterogeneous device fleet in a way that once seemed reserved for the largest enterprises with custom-built systems.

Ultimately, the spotlight turned toward the future of Intune and Azure AD, underscoring how rapidly evolving features, driven by AI and machine learning, are reshaping the entire field of security. The principle of continuous adaptation stood out as central—nobody can afford to "set and forget" their policies. Whether it's an emerging OS, a zero-day exploit, or a regulatory change, the only constant is change itself. Staying aware of Microsoft's roadmap, engaging with the user community, and proactively testing new functionalities ensure that your environment doesn't just survive in the face of transformation, but thrives.

Applying Knowledge in Real-World Environments

From theory and technical details to real-world case studies, this book has aimed to equip you with tools for action. Now comes the practical step: translating these lessons into tangible improvements in your own organization. Whether you're an IT manager, a security professional, or a team lead tasked with endpoint compliance, consider the following approaches as you move forward:

1. **Revisit Your Current Policies**
   Before piling on new rules, examine your existing ones. Check for overlap, conflicts, or outdated settings that no longer align with your organization's needs. Sometimes, it helps to start with a blank slate: if you were implementing Intune policies from scratch today, would your existing setup look the same? Identifying gaps can yield quick wins, like consolidating multiple policies into one coherent rule set or removing a requirement that confuses more than it protects.

2. **Map Out a Pilot Strategy**
   If you plan to adopt advanced features or revamp your conditional access rules, do so incrementally. Select a pilot group that represents the diversity of your workforce—remote workers, office-based staff, BYOD advocates, and so forth. Observe how they respond to the new policies, gather feedback, then refine. This iterative process can save countless hours of crisis management when the new settings roll out organization-wide.

3. **Leverage Integration Points**
   Integrating Intune more deeply with Azure AD, Microsoft Defender for Endpoint, or other Microsoft 365 services can reduce manual oversight and speed up threat response. Consider automating remediation steps for certain common issues or raising real-time alerts whenever a device hits a high-risk status. These capabilities reduce the burden on IT staff, freeing them for strategic tasks rather than firefighting.

4. **Document and Communicate**
   Communication isn't just for problem-solving—it's vital for successful policy deployment. Keeping employees informed about what changes are coming, why they matter, and how they'll

be affected helps build trust. Clear documentation ensures that every stakeholder, from executives to end users, can reference the "how" and "why" behind each policy. This not only smooths adoption but also helps new team members quickly understand the environment.

By combining these strategies, you can harness the full power of Intune to safeguard your organization's data while still providing the flexibility modern workforces demand. Always remember that security and productivity need not be at odds; when implemented thoughtfully, compliance and conditional access create an environment that encourages safe, efficient work, rather than hampering it.

Fostering a Culture of Adaptation

The knowledge you've gained here isn't static—nor should it be. The cybersecurity landscape shifts daily, and your environment will evolve as employees adopt new devices, apps, and work patterns. A crucial takeaway is that your security strategy must keep pace. That implies a few key commitments:

- **Stay Informed**: Subscribe to Microsoft's release notes, follow technology blogs, and engage with user communities. Small changes in Microsoft's service updates can have big implications for your policies.

- **Remain Flexible**: If a new device type or OS emerges, be ready to test and adapt. Strict, unyielding policies risk hindering legitimate work. A culture that embraces change sees new challenges as opportunities to refine and strengthen security measures.

- **Encourage Feedback**: Employees on the ground often spot issues before administrators do. Cultivate an atmosphere where users feel comfortable reporting friction or confusion with policies. Use these insights to refine your rules and better align them with real-world workflows.

- **Invest in Ongoing Education**: For both IT professionals and the broader workforce, awareness and training are essential. The more people understand why a policy exists, the more likely they are to comply and spot threats before damage occurs.

Looking Beyond the Horizon

As Microsoft continues to integrate AI, analytics, and automation into Intune and Azure AD, the line between endpoint management and holistic cybersecurity will blur further. You can anticipate a future where devices self-correct minor security lapses, adapt to user roles on the fly, and even learn from patterns across the entire ecosystem—an era that might see the manual creation of policies replaced by AI-suggested baselines and real-time risk assessments. While this shift promises to reduce much of the administrative overhead, it also underscores the importance of human oversight, creativity, and ethical considerations. The more powerful the tools become, the more we need skilled, reflective professionals to guide them.

In this sense, your journey doesn't end with closing these pages. Instead, think of it as a stepping stone, a foundation that prepares you for the next wave of developments. Whether you're delving into advanced threat analytics, exploring cross-platform device management, or helping design your organization's zero-trust framework, the core principles of well-structured compliance and real-time conditional access will remain indispensable. You're now equipped to take those principles further, tailoring them to meet whatever complexities lie ahead.

Your Role in Driving Security Forward

Through reading this book, you've demonstrated a commitment not just to learning the mechanics of Intune, but to reimagining how your organization handles security. That puts you in a pivotal position. Your willingness to champion best practices, test new features, and share successes or challenges with your peers can influence an entire corporate culture. Whether you're a one-person IT team at a startup or part of a global department in a multinational, your insights and initiatives can ripple outward, shaping how data is protected at every level.

So, as you depart this journey, remember that your understanding of Intune's capabilities and philosophy places you among those best suited to drive meaningful, adaptable security. Continue to refine your knowledge, welcome fresh ideas, and question assumptions that no longer serve you. By doing so, you stand as a catalyst for excellence in endpoint management, forging a world where compliance isn't a burdensome checklist, but a cohesive strategy that supports innovation, collaboration, and a futureproof posture against threats yet to emerge.

As you apply these lessons and push the boundaries of what Intune can do, you'll find that security becomes less of a hurdle and more of a strategic ally. When done right, it empowers employees to work productively from any device, fosters trust among clients and partners, and can even serve as a competitive differentiator. The true journey of compliance and conditional access is one of continuous adaptation—an ongoing venture that you now have the tools and inspiration to lead. Go forth, embrace these challenges, and guide your organization into a future where secure, intelligent, and dynamic endpoint management is the norm rather than the exception.

www.ingramcontent.com/pod-product-compliance
Lightning Source LLC
LaVergne TN
LVHW051705050326
832903LV00032B/4022